The Four-Seven Debate

SUNY *Series in Korean Studies*
Sung Bae Park, Editor

THE FOUR-SEVEN DEBATE

AN ANNOTATED TRANSLATION OF THE MOST FAMOUS CONTROVERSY IN KOREAN NEO-CONFUCIAN THOUGHT

MICHAEL C. KALTON

WITH

OAKSOOK C. KIM,
SUNG BAE PARK,
YOUNGCHAN RO,
TU WEI-MING,
AND
SAMUEL YAMASHITA

STATE UNIVERSITY OF NEW YORK PRESS

Published by
State University of New York Press, Albany

For information, address State University of New York
Press, State University Plaza, Albany, N.Y., 12246

Production by Diane Ganeles
Marketing by Theresa Swierzowski

Library of Congress Cataloging-in-Publication Data

Kalton, Michael C.
    The four-seven debate : an annotated translation of the most
famous controversy in Korean neo-confucian thought / by Michael C.
Kalton ; with Oaksook C. Kim . . . [et al.].
        p.   cm. — (SUNY series in Korean studies)
    Includes bibliographical references.
    ISBN 0-7914-1751-4 (alk. paper)—ISBN 0-7914-1752-2
(pbk.: alk. paper)
    1. Four beginnings and seven feelings thesis. 2. Neo-
Confucianism—Korea. 3. Philosophers, Korean—Correspondence.
I. Kim, Oaksook Chun. II. Title. III. Series.
B5253.F68K35   1994
181'.119—dc20   93-12299
                                                                       CIP

10 9 8 7 6 5 4 3 2 1

Contents

Translator's Preface

The complete correspondence between T'oegye and Kobong on the Four-Seven Debate was compiled into a single volume and widely circulated; this volume was eventually incorporated into *Kobong chŏnjip* (The Complete Collected Works of Ki Taesŭng), which was photo reprinted by Sŏnggyun'gwan University in 1976. The text found in the Sŏnggyun'gwan edition of *Yulgok chŏnsŏ* (The Complete Works of Yi I) has been used for the correspondence between Yulgok and Ugye.

To facilitate cross-referencing the translation and for ease of reference to the original, the pagination of the original texts has been preserved and is indicated by boldface numbering on the left-hand side of the page.

Writings for an educated audience in premodern Korea were in literary Chinese, which is the language of these texts. Korean pronounciation of the characters, however, differs from that of the Chinese. Names of persons, titles of works, and so on, that are Chinese are rendered according to their Chinese pronunciation following the modified Wade-Giles system of romanization. Korean names, titles, and technical terms romanized in the text are rendered according to the Korean pronunciation, following the simplified McCune-Reischauer system developed by Professor Gari Ledyard of Columbia University. An exception, however, is the term "principle" (Kor. *i*, Chin. *li*). The initial l (or r) reappears in the Korean pronounciation in medial positions when the character is used in compounds, and the term *li* is thoroughly familiar to the scholarly community dealing with Neo-Confucian thought; thus I have chosen to retain that form.

Acknowledgments

The foundation for this volume was laid through an extraordinarily pleasant and fruitful academic collaboration. For over four years six of us (four from the Korean field, one each from China and Japan) met annually to work on this material. We divided the text among us; each brought his or her assigned portion to the meeting, where we went over the translations and discussed both translation questions and the philosophical content of the texts. During the intervening months, I edited the translations from the previous session and distributed the reworked version at the next meeting. In addition to me, the members of our "Four-Seven Group" included Oaksook C. Kim (UCLA); Sung Bae Park (SUNY at Stony Brook); Youngchan Ro (George Mason University); Tu Wei-ming (Harvard University); and Samuel Yamashita (Pomona College). We are most grateful to the Joint Committee on Korean Studies of the Social Science Research Council and the American Council of Learned Societies for the support that made our meetings possible.

All translation is an interpretive act, and especially with texts such as these choices of rendering, are deeply informed by one's view of the philosophical issues at hand. The original translations have by now been reworked repeatedly, so the final choice of words and the interpretation behind them must be my responsibility. At the same time, my own understanding is inextricably entwined with the discussions of our group, and I hope our collective wisdom has not been too badly distorted as it was refracted through my final lens.

I would like to thank Columbia University Press for permission to reprint portions of this material that appeared in *Sources of Korean Tradition* (1992), edited by Peter Lee with Donald Baker, Yongho Ch'oe, Hugh H. W. Kang and Han-Kyo Kim. And, finally, I would like to express my appreciation to Wichita State University, which supported my final revision of this manuscript with a Faculty Summer Research Grant.

Abbreviations

Introduction
to the Four-Seven Debate

Two of the most famous names in Korean history are those of T'oegye (Yi Hwang, 1501–1570) and Yulgok (Yi I, 1536–1584). In twentieth-century Korea they have become national symbols, figures that inspire pride and confidence in a cultural tradition both long and rich. Intellectual currents stemming from them mingled with regional politics and factional identities in subsequent generations, giving rise to partisan lineages of a kind that they themselves would have disavowed. But above all the famous controversy associated with them, the "Four-Seven Debate," addressed issues at the core of the great Ch'eng-Chu¹ synthesis in a way that set an important and distinctive philosophic agenda for subsequent generations of Korean thinkers.

Just as every Korean knows about T'oegye and Yulgok, most have also heard of the Four-Seven Debate. But while the thinkers have become emblems of national pride, the intellectual exchange that established their position at the center of Korean Neo-Confucian thought has become almost a byword for abstruse and difficult philosophizing. Now only specialists can grasp the issues and understand why they were of such gripping interest and importance.

This marks the divide between contemporary Korea and a past in which Koreans boasted of being the world's bulwark of orthodox Neo-Confucianism. Values, customs, and deep assumptions about man and the world have carried over from this Neo-Confucian past to transform Korea's modernity. But in the past this world view and value system were crystalized into a sophisticated and articulate philosophy. Known as "the study of the nature and principle" (*sŏngnihak*), this learning encompassed metaphysics, cosmology, and philosophy of man in the scope of a unified anthropocosmic vision. Its practical aim was the cultivation of character, and it developed a sophisticated ascetical theory combining both intellectual and meditative pursuits.

At the very center of *sŏngnihak* stands the metaphysically based description of the structure and functioning of the human psyche. Upon this description the whole structure of theory converged, for it was the intellectual link between theory and practice, and the concern for the actual practice of self-cultivation was the animating wellspring of the entire system. It is because the Four-Seven Debate involves key issues at the heart of this central body of psychological theory that T'oegye, Yulgok, and Korean Neo-Confucians for centuries after regarded it as a matter of the utmost importance. And it is the loss of this explicit philosophical structure that makes its significance difficult to understand—"empty speculation," to many in the modern world.

Because of the theoretical and practical centrality of psychological theory in Neo-Confucian thought, it is also the area of greatest complexity. The great synthesis welded together by Chu Hsi (1130–1200) in China's Sung dynasty joined together elements of creative advances made by his immediate predecessors as they revived and reappropriated a tradition for centuries overshadowed by Taoism and Buddhism. From the Ch'eng brothers[2] came the dualistic philosophy of principle (*li*) and material force (*ki*, Chin. *ch'i*), and their uncle Chang Tsai (1020–1077) introduced the notion of a *ki*-based "physical nature" that provided a hitherto lacking explanation for evil. The overarching metaphysical framework came from Chou Tun-i (1017–1073), whose *Diagram of the Supreme Ultimate* served as a monistic interpretive vehicle for the *li/ki* dualism. Terminology for a newly elaborated description of the inner life and structure of the mind was borrowed largely from the classic *Mencius*, which provided the major passages used to validate the new insights, and the newly classic *Doctrine of the Mean* contributed a foundation for meditative discipline. These developments occupied the foreground; in the background was a more subtle meeting of great world traditions as the Taoist and Buddhist ambience contributed its own notes to this surge of Confucian vitality and creativity.[3]

In the eyes of Neo-Confucian scholars such as T'oegye and Yulgok, the work of Chu Hsi and the Ch'engs was an insightful reappropriation of the authoritative teaching of the sages. Points of error and misinterpretation might have crept in—especially among the many disciples of the Sung dynasty masters—but there could be no question as to whether the whole was sufficiently coherent; apparent contradictions or difficulties were only a challenge to further thought and insight. The question was not whether but how it all fit together. T'oegye and Yulgok were both eloquent advocates of a flexible approach that could tolerate and embrace the great disparity evident among even the most authoritative sources.

The intellectual historian, however, approaches a synthesis that encompasses such diversity of time, place, culture, and religion with a suspicion that it will include as well a measure of tension, if not outright contradiction. Korea is uniquely suited for the pursuit of such questions, for the Chosŏn dynasty (1392–1910) was the only society that over the centuries maintained a virtually exclusive loyalty to the orthodox Ch'eng-Chu school of Neo-Confucianism.

When there is a prolonged and general loyalty to any complex philosophy, philosophical discourse tends to take on the character of fine-grained, exacting analysis and argumentation known as "scholasticism." This is a treasure for those interested in discovering the dynamic tensions and stresses that reveal the structural seams of a complex philosophical synthesis. As the fine grain emerges in a piece of wood through long polishing, so too does scholastic polishing inevitably bring out the fine grain of the system. And it is the controversies that resist solution that are most of interest: if there is some point that can engage fine minds on both sides for decades or even centuries, it likely indicates a deeper strain, conflict, or tension in the very structure of the system itself.

Seen in this light, one might well expect the Four-Seven Debate to provide a unique window on the complex "study of the nature and principle" of the dominant Ch'eng-Chu tradition of

Neo-Confucianism. It is uniquely focused on the complex psychological theory at the core of Ch'eng-Chu learning, engaged the preeminent thinkers, and it continued for centuries with no final resolution.

Background

Historical Development of Neo-Confucianism in Korea

When Chu Hsi died in 1200, his political opponents were in the ascendant, and the future of his great synthesis was, at best, uncertain. It was more than a century later, under a very different kind of political auspices, that the Ch'eng-Chu school first attained the definitive institutional centrality in Chinese society that it was to enjoy for centuries. China had fallen to the Mongols who established the short-lived Yüan dynasty (1279–1368). In 1313, when they reestablished the Chinese civil service examination system, Chu Hsi's version of the classics and his commentaries became the official canon for the examinations. This meant that henceforth aspirants for coveted careers as government officials would necessarily become versed in Ch'eng-Chu learning.

As a means to legitimize their rule in China, the Mongols deliberately set about internationalizing the bureaucracy. The brief Yüan dynasty was thus a uniquely cosmopolitan period, and many Koreans were among the foreigners who studied in China, took the examinations, and began their careers in government there. Both An Hyang (1243–1313) and Paek Ijŏng (?), the men credited with first introducing Neo-Confucianism to the Korean peninsula, studied it first while in residence at the Yüan capital. It became common for the sons of the Korean aristocracy to finish their education in China, and as they returned they carried with them the new learning and its most fundamental texts.

Korea's Koryŏ dynasty (918–1392) had been founded under Buddhist auspices. By the latter half of the fourteenth century, however, the government was in a state of fiscal crisis, and the wealth, land, slaves, and manpower absorbed by Buddhist temples made the Buddhist establishment a tempting and vulnerable target. At first, the Neo-Confucian learning trickling in from Yüan China was treated as a mundane complement to Buddhism, a body of appropriate lore for those involved in government. This followed a modus vivendi established between the traditions since their introduction to the peninsula in the late fourth century. But the situation changed as the new learning took root among young officials, and the fiscal crisis steadily deepened. The new learning gradually began to assume the proportions of an independent power base: criticism of Buddhist excess and calls for reform began to be supplanted by more radical voices criticizing it in principle as an erroneous doctrine that should be suppressed. The revolution that placed General Yi Sŏnggye on the throne as the founder of a new dynasty in 1392 was accomplished with the support of a group of young Neo-Confucian officials. The Chosŏn dynasty (1392–1910) became the first and only East Asian regime to be established under exclusive Neo-Confucian auspices.

In China, the Mongols had been recently replaced by the Chinese Ming dynasty (1368–1662). The Ming court was at first quite suspicious about the upheaval in Korea, and only after considerable delay did Yi Sŏnggye win official Chinese sanction for his new regime. The relationship remained strained throughout the next century, reversing the constant interchange that had characterized the Yüan era. As Korean scholars worked to deepen their comprehension of the complex Neo-Confucian synthesis, they did so with relatively little contact or respect for Ming scholarship. Instead, a distinctive pattern of referring almost wholly to Chu Hsi, the Ch'eng brothers, and other authoritative Sung dynasty sources was set in place. When the new interpretations introduced by Wang Yang-ming (1472–1529) swept China and even overshadowed the Ch'eng-Chu school, Korea was already sufficiently distanced and intellectually independent to prove largely resistant to the tide of the times. When the "barbarian" Manchus overwhelmed the Ming and established the Ch'ing dynasty in the mid-seventeenth century, the intellectual divide became even more marked: the Koreans self-confidently pronounced themselves the sole guardians of the True Learning. In no other East Asian society did the Ch'eng-Chu school of thought enjoy such exclusive attention or intensive development.

Creative intellectual development of the tradition was not the first order of the day, however. The first century of the new dynasty was largely a time of institution building, as the new dynasty established its political and social character. The potentials of the Ch'eng-Chu vision were bifurcated, as busy bureaucrats attended to government affairs at the center, while those ousted for one reason or another from the power struggles at the center taught and pursued the intensive self-cultivation dimensions of Neo-Confucian learning in the countryside. The division was to prove explosive. As scholars from the countryside began to find their way back into government, the entrenched and powerful establishment figures in the highest reaches of the bureaucracy increasingly came under strong moralistic attack.

The moral idealism and even rigor inherent in Neo-Confucianism found ample voice in no less than three offices of the government bureaucracy that had the power of remonstrance. When these offices acted in concert on an issue, they could paralyze the government and thwart the will of even the king. The tension between the power of remonstrance and the ability of the ruler and his high councilors to set policy came to a disastrous climax in the bloody "literati purges" that marred the first two decades of the sixteenth century. The worst of these visited torture and death throughout the ranks of officialdom on anyone who had had any connection with criticism or remonstrance. This occurred in the reign of Yŏnsan'gun (1495–1506), who descended from paranoia into true madness before he was deposed. His successor, King Chungjong (1506–1544), had to compensate by being as tolerant of criticism as Yŏnsan'gun had been intolerant, and soon a moralistic crusade to make his reign a return of the golden age of sage rule was under way. Idealistic young officials led by the charismatic Cho Kwangjo (1482–1519) again pushed the ruler and high ministers too far too fast: the last of the literati purges, in 1519, cost Cho his life and gave Korean officialdom an exemplary martyr.

The literati purges became an important symbolic reference point, leaving a distinctive impression on Korean Neo-Confucianism. The strongly self-cultivation–oriented and morally rigorous strain of Ch'eng-Chu Neo-Confucianism known as the Learning of the Way (Kor. *tohak*, Chin. *tao-hsüeh*), with this impetus, became a particularly pronounced feature of the Korean tradition. The participants in the Four-Seven Debate were all earnest *tohak* practitioners. The great concern they evince for subtle distinctions in the complex system of Ch'eng-Chu anthropocosmic psychological theory is itself grounded in this *tohak*: what may seem like theory to us was to them an urgent matter of correctly apprehending the essential framework for the ascetical theory guiding the practice of self-cultivation. Nothing in the intellectual life could be more important.

The havoc of the literati purges has left us scant record of the intellectual life of the period. The earliest thinkers of the Koryŏ-Chosŏn transition period such as Kwŏn Kŭn (1352–1409) and Chŏng Tojŏn (?–1398) showed a good grasp of metaphysical theory, but evidenced little concern for the meditative dimensions of self-cultivation practice that were an important Neo-Confucian development. Remarks concerning the idealistic movement surrounding Cho Kwangjo a century later reflect, on the contrary, a strong emphasis on self-cultivation and meditative discipline, almost to the exclusion of the "book learning" that provided the framework of metaphysical-psychological theory for balanced practice. After the purge of 1519, a shadow hung over the earnest self-cultivation *tohak* side of Neo-Confucianism, which again seemed shunted to the periphery. But the seesaw experience of bifurcation and overemphasis was gradually yielding a more balanced grasp of the whole. The flowering of a mature and full understanding of the complex and many-layered Neo-Confucian synthesis came by the middle of the century.

The advent of maturity in Korean Neo-Confucian thought is associated above all with the name of T'oegye. Born in the dark years of the mad Yŏnsan'gun, still a youth in the heyday of Cho Kwangjo's idealistic movement, his years as a government official were spent in the dispirited atmosphere that was the aftermath of the purge of 1519. His bent was for learning, self-cultivation, and solitude, and by 1549 he had retired to a life of study and teaching. But he grasped with a clarity and theoretical force not to be found earlier the balance between the active and the quiet that runs throughout all aspects of Ch'eng-Chu thought. He did his utmost to avoid the numerous summons to return to active service, yielding briefly only when the pressure became intolerable. But in the next decades his disciples began filling the government as the post-purge atmosphere cleared with the accession of a new ruler.

It was at this point of early full flourishing that, in 1559, the issues of the Four-Seven Debate were joined between T'oegye and a young scholar-official, Ki Taesŭng (Kobong, 1527–1572). In raising and minutely examining the complex conceptual issues at the junction between the metaphysical structure of the cosmos and the functioning of the human psyche, the Four-Seven Debate reached a new state of the art in Ch'eng-Chu thought and established a template for the kind of issues and concerns that became the hallmark of Korean Neo-Confucian theory for centuries to come.

Elements of Ch'eng-Chu Psychological Theory

The Four-Seven Debate involves the status of various kinds of feelings in their relation to human nature and in particular with respect to the metaphysical composition (*li* and *ki*, principle and material force) of the psyche within which they arise. First, therefore, we need to consider the orthodox view on matters such as the psyche, nature, and feelings, and then we will look in more detail at their metaphysical composition.

Sim (Chin. *hsin*), variously translated as "mind" or "mind-and-heart," is the Neo-Confucian term for the seat of consciousness; with our *sim* we have feelings or desires, thoughts, and resolves. The perennial Chinese approach was to pose questions about human activity situationally: activity, including the life of the psyche, was basically seen as occurring as a response to one's situation or surroundings. In line with this, the feelings were viewed as the mind-and-heart's most fundamental form of activity. The initial response to a given situation, in this view, is a natural or spontaneous feeling such as anger, joy, fear, or desire, which then leads to further activity such as thoughtful consideration or intentions.

In this situational perspective, the most fundamental moral question would be the appropriateness or inappropriateness of one's response. Ideally, one's feelings would be spontaneously or naturally appropriate, a direct guide for action with no need for careful thought and control. However, this happy condition belonged only to the fully perfect, the sages. For ordinary mortals, emphasis was placed on the exercise of careful reflection and discernment; the Neo-Confucians fomulated the exercise of this governance as the particular office of the mind-and-heart. The focus, however, remained on cultivating an ever more perfectly attuned responsiveness and purifying whatever might cause distortions in one's response.

Here we must pause to consider what makes a response appropriate and what makes it inappropriate; giving an explicit account of this was an achievement that took the Neo-Confucians beyond all earlier Confucian theory. The resources from which their answer was drawn were in part the perennial East Asian world view and in part new ideas with a somewhat Buddhist imprint.

Appropriateness supposes some kind of unity. The Neo-Confucian understanding in this regard was in line with the widely shared East Asian assumptions most clearly crystalized in Taoist thought: the one Tao, a structuring, guiding and normative pattern, runs through all things just as a single pattern governs and informs all the interacting and interdependent parts of a single living body. The Tao is at once the nature of all things and the nature of each particular thing, depending on what level you look at it. The Neo-Confucians could and did use the traditional term "Tao," but more often they used another term, *li*, "principle," to convey the same thought. Like the Tao, principle, "is one, but manifested diversely," constitutes the inner nature of all things, and is the one all-encompassing and normative nature of everything. In this last sense, it is called the "Supreme Ultimate," a term derived from Chou Tun-i's *Diagram of Supreme Ultimate*, which itself derived originally from Taoist sources. Because this *li*, which is the nature of all things, is also fully present as the inner structure or nature of the mind-and-heart, human beings are equipped to respond appropriately to all things. *Li* being itself the norm of appropriateness or goodness, man's nature can be described as purely good, and this was understood as supporting and explicating the traditional Mencian contention that human nature is good.

The notion of the Tao, or *li* as Tao, explicates appropriateness and the norm for what is appropriate. What it does not do is explain deviance. Traditional explanations, Confucian and Taoist alike, always explained this in terms of selfishness or self-centeredness, a clear violation of the appropriate corporate unity among persons and things. But Tao/*li* explains appropriateness on the level of metaphysical structure, while selfishness belongs to the level of moral phenomena. In other words, an equivalent explanation for deviance was lacking.

The creative move of the Neo-Confucians at this point was to pair *li* dualistically with another constituent of all concrete beings, *ki* (Chin. *ch'i*), "material force." The term itself was not new; it had a long tradition of usage with varied and overlapping meanings—the vital force of life itself, the force of the feelings, breath, the atmosphere, or the basic stuff of the whole universe. In Neo-Confucian usage, *ki* is the concretizing and energizing component in all psychic or physical being, both personal and cosmic.

As the psychophysical component of beings, then, there is nothing particularly novel about *ki*. Traditionally, Tao is simply the pattern inherent in *ki*, and *ki* is the concrete vehicle in which the Tao is realized; the terms are two, but they are complementary to the point of being virtually monistic. Such was the philosophical system of Chang Tsai, and a similar view is implicit in Chou Tun-i's *Diagram*. In Korea, Sŏ Kyŏngdŏk (Hwadam, 1489–1546) is famous as an exponent of this approach.

The mainstream of Neo-Confucian thought, however, was set on quite a different path by the Ch'eng brothers, who introduced a dualistic treatment of *li* and *ki*; Chu Hsi followed them in this and assimilated the contributions of Chang and Chou to the new framework. The fundamental importance of this contribution is recognized in the appellation the "Ch'eng-Chu school" rather than simply the "Chu Hsi school."

The Ch'engs and Chu Hsi continued the tradition that described *li* and *ki* as totally complementary and interdependent. But they modified this tradition by adding to *ki* an ambiguous limiting/ distorting function associated with its varying degrees of purity and turbidity, fineness and coarseness. As limiting, *Ki*'s variations explained the different degrees or kinds of creatures, from the most blocked up and turbid inanimate objects to the sensitive and seemingly unlimited capacity for response found in human beings. As a distorting factor, the same turbidity explained how, in spite of the perfection of human nature (*li*), the psychophysical component (*ki*) could disrupt the appropriate responsiveness rooted in the depths of our nature. With this, the traditional Mencian doctrine of the goodness of human nature was interpreted as meaning that our "original nature" (*li*) is perfectly good, but our "physical nature" (*li* as subject to the imperfection of *ki*) is problematic unless one enjoys the perfectly pure psychophysical endowment characteristic of a sage.

This was a decisive advance for Confucian thought; for the first time, it was possible to give a plausible philosophical explanation for the distorting selfish tendencies that beset human beings. Mencius was right: human nature (as *li*) is good. But in the murky patterns of thought and affectivity that hardly break beyond the enclosing confines of self-concern, a psychophysical turbidity is evident that distorts and disrupts our appropriate connection with the world around us.

But what is the significance of the Mencian doctrine in this context? Does the doctrine of the original nature do anything but preserve Mencius's intent verbally? Is not the physical nature with its admitted imperfection and limitation the only functional reality? As we shall see, the status of Mencius is central to the Four-Seven Debate: The "four" of the Four-Seven refers to the four inherently good dispositions he cited as evidence of the goodness of human nature, and the essence of the controversy concerns how this should be understood in the context of the *li/ki* dualism of the physical nature doctrine.

The dualistic treatment of *li* and *ki* moved several pairs of contrasting terms into prominence in Ch'eng-Chu thought. The "original nature" and the "physical nature" we have already seen; they are important reference points throughout the first phase of the Four-Seven Debate, that between T'oegye and Kobong. In the next round, when, after T'oegye's death, Yulgok and his friend Ugye (Sŏng Hon, 1535–1598) resurrected the issue, a similar pair, the "Tao mind" and the "human mind" become the focus of attention. The general use of such dichotomous terminology easily accented the dualistic aspect of Ch'eng-Chu thought.

The immediate topic in the Four-Seven Debate involves the various kinds of feelings and the way they originate. Neo-Confucians conceptualized this question in terms of a "substance-function" relationship. The latent structure of our existence, the nature (*li*), is "substance." As such, it cannot be directly observed. In the concrete, active phenomenal world, the constitution of our nature is manifested in the way we respond to things, that is, in the life of the feelings. They are described as "function" in relation to nature as substance.

This way of conceiving the relationship of the nature and the feelings is intimately connected with *li-ki* metaphysics: the nature is pure *li*, but feelings belong to the concrete phenomenal world, that is, the world of *ki*, or more precisely, of *li* embodied and concretized in *ki*. Thus the question of the origin of good (appropriate) versus less appropriate or reliable sorts of feeling-responses is a lever for prying out the subtlest implications of one's view of *li* and *ki*.

Li is the norm and source of appropriateness, while *ki* accounts for distortion. Since feelings are necessarily a combination of the two, the *li-ki* theory seems on the face of it a good explanation for how feelings sometimes hit and sometimes miss the mark, and such was the general Ch'eng-Chu understanding of the matter. But if one supposes that there are some feelings that tend of themselves to be correct and that there are others so liable to stray that they call for the greatest watchfulness, then one might well question whether such disparities might be rooted in different configurations of the relationship of such feelings to *li* and *ki*. This is precisely the question that gave rise to the Four-Seven Debate.

The Four-Seven Debate

In Neo-Confucian thought, there was a conventional list of feelings taken from a passage in the *Book of Rites* that symbolized the feelings in general. These were the so-called Seven Feelings: desire, hate, love, fear, grief, anger, and joy.[4] In a passage of critical importance to Neo-Confucian psychological and ascetical theory, the first chapter of the *Doctrine of the Mean* gave a shorter list, which was considered simply an abbreviated reference to the Seven Feelings:

> The condition before joy, anger, grief, or pleasure are aroused is called equilibrium; after they are aroused and each attains proper measure, it is called harmony. Equilibrium is the great foundation of the universe; harmony is its universal path.

Insofar as the mention of "proper measure" implies that at times proper measure may be wanting, this passage is taken as a clear indication that the Seven Feelings are mixed or indeterminate, sometimes good and sometimes bad.

In an equally important and famous passage, however, Mencius introduces the "Four Beginnings" in support of his argument that human nature is good:

> From this one can see that if one does not have the disposition of commiseration, he is not human; if he does not have the disposition of shame and dislike [for evil], he is not human; if he does not have the disposition of yielding and deference, he is not human; if he does not have the disposition of approving [the good] and disapproving [evil], he is not human. The disposition of compassion is the beginning of humanity, the disposition of shame and dislike is the beginning of righteousness, the disposition of yielding and deference is the beginning of propriety, the disposition of approving and disapproving is the beginning of wisdom.[5]

Mencius seems to have had an organic growth perspective: we have these four inherent good dispositions that, if nurtured, will develop into the fully mature qualities of humanity, righteousness, propriety, and wisdom. In the context of a substance-function framework and *li-ki* philosophy, Neo-Confucians read it with a somewhat different twist, however. Humanity, righteousness, propriety, and wisdom are *li*, the components of the nature that is the substance of the mind-and-heart; the Four Beginnings are the correlated feelings that manifest the nature. They are "beginnings" not in the sense of sprouts or seedlings, but like the initial clue one picks up as the track of something hidden; this interpretation was facilitated by the fact that the character Mencius used for "beginning" was *tan* (Chin. *tuan*), literally the beginning/end of a piece of thread.

In classical passages that were among the most fundamental pillars of Neo-Confucian thought, then, are embedded references to feelings that may or may not be good (the Seven Feelings) and feelings so evidently good that they serve as indicators of the inherent goodness of the nature (the Four Beginnings). The question is, does this represent two kinds of feelings, or is it just two different ways of speaking about the feelings? If it is the former, perhaps there is some sort of difference in the way they arise in the *li-ki* composite of our psyche. This has an initial plausibility, since the essential difference between the Four and Seven seems to be the pure goodness (associated with *li*) of the former and the vulnerability to distortion (a matter of *ki*) of the latter. However, this interpretation so emphasizes the dualistic view of *li* and *ki* that the overall monistic framework demanding their fundamental complementary and absolute interdependence is threatened.

Such was the shape the question soon assumed when the controversy was joined between T'oegye and Kobong.

The T'oegye-Kobong Debate

The seed of the Four-Seven Debate was sown in 1553 when T'oegye was helping Chŏng Chiun (1509–1561) emend his "Diagram of the Heavenly Mandate" (*Chŏnmyŏng to*).[6] Among many changes, T'oegye introduced the expression "The Four Beginnings are the issuance of principle; the Seven Feelings are the issuance of material force." T'oegye meant for this to tone down the dualism of a very similar expression Chŏng had used, but he later heard that Kobong had spoken critically of this outright splitting of feelings between *li* and *ki*. He wrote to Kobong in 1559 suggesting a further slight modification; Kobong replied with a more detailed three-page critique of the whole approach. This prompted T'oegye to address the matter much more seriously, and in an eight-page letter he made his first attempt to lay out his thinking fully. Kobong responded with a forty-two-page, paragraph by paragraph critique of T'oegye's letter.

This time T'oegye sent back another draft of his eight-page letter, carefully corrected in line with what he accepted of Kobong's critique. But that was not all: He accompanied the new draft with forty-six pages of point-by-point response to Kobong's long critique. Kobong again wrote a lengthy reply; on many points they had reached agreement, but significant differences remained. T'oegye's reply was brief, essentially politely declining to continue the argument; he felt that much had been learned but that there was nothing to be gained by trying to force some final agreement. After three or four years of further consideration, Kobong wrote a general summary statement of the issue; there may have remained important differences beneath the surface, but Kobong's summation seemed in basic harmony with T'oegye's position. The year was probably 1566, some seven years since the discussion had begun.[7]

This protracted interchange produced a unique body of correspondence: the continuity of the discourse, the complexity, detail, and careful process of point-by-point argumentation, reasoned agreement and disagreement, and development and modification of initial positions is simply unparalleled in Neo-Confucian literature. The interchange itself between a very senior scholar and statesman and a young man at the beginning of his career is also highly unusual. Kobong, some twenty-six years younger than T'oegye, was taking extraordinary liberties in his frank and direct challenge and critique of T'oegye's ideas; in the age-conscious and rigidly hierarchical society of the times, this was almost unthinkable. And T'oegye's response was totally in line with rarely practiced Confucian ideals: He was indeed willing to listen to anyone, however junior, and modify his opinions in the light of what he heard. Kobong, in his courageous forthrightness, and T'oegye, in his tolerance, flexibility, and intellectual humility, exemplified a level of intellectual interaction rarely attained.

The text speaks for itself. Because it is so lengthy, portions that were peripheral discussions have been omitted, but the core arguments have been presented in full. Since point-by-point discussion and response became the format for this interchange, extensive annotation cross-referencing the letters has been introduced. To facilitate both cross-referencing and consultation of the original text, boldface page numbers at the lefthand margin indicate the pagination of the original manuscript, and cross-referencing within this volume uses the pagination of the original.

The Yulgok-Ugye Debate

T'oegye died in 1570, and Kobong passed away just two years later. Their debate was already well-known, however, and the manuscript circulated as a separate volume before it was eventually incorporated into Kobong's collected works. The issue that had seemed resolved in its pages, however, was resurrected in 1572, the very year of Kobong's death.

The occasion that gave rise to the second round of the debate was a letter written in 1572 by Ugye to his good friend Yulgok (Yi I). Ugye had been reading T'oegye, and at the same time his attention had been caught by a passage in Chu Hsi's famous preface to the *Doctrine of the Mean*. In it, Chu Hsi differentiates the Tao mind and the human mind as "the one arises from the individuality (*ssu*) of the psychophysical endowment while the other originates in the correctness of the normative nature."[8] Ugye and Yulgok had formerly been in agreement that T'oegye was overly dualistic and that Kobong in fact had been correct, but now this evident parallel with T'oegye's analysis of the differing origin of the Four Beginnings and Seven Feelings inclined him to reconsider the plausibility of T'oegye's position. Yulgok responded with a letter meant to settle the matter, but it was not to be so easily laid to rest.

We have in all five letters of Ugye's and six responses from Yulgok. Ugye's letters average about four or five folio pages, while Yulgok's are double that. Unlike the lengthy period of the T'oegye-Kobong correspondence, the Ugye-Yulgok interchange proceeded with great intensity over a relatively brief period of time and was completed within the year. The character of the correspondence is also quite different. Kobong had followed a careful point-by-point process in critiquing T'oegye's discussion, and T'oegye had responded in kind. Equal in age and close friends, Ugye and Yulgok are not so formal in their process. Ugye expresses doubts and reservations; unlike Kobong's challenging critique, he draws Yulgok on to further heights by refusing to be convinced. Thus as one tack after another fails to accomplish its purpose, Yulgok moves from directly addressing the issue to reviewing and synthesizing the framework of Ch'eng-Chu metaphysics and finally to introducing his own creative reconceptualization of the essence of the entire system.

The richness in the T'oegye-Kobong debate is to be found by moving between them, seeing the systematic tensions revealed as they develop their alternative perspectives. The Ugye-Yulgok round is equally rich, but in a different way. Although Ugye does make some good points, the main focus here is clearly Yulgok, one of the Neo-Confucian tradition's most brilliant systematic thinkers. Ugye's entertaining the plausibility of a dualistic interpretation of Chu Hsi's system put the onus on Yulgok to explicate convincingly both the metaphysical concepts and their psycho-moral application in a consistently nondualistic manner. In T'oegye-Kobong, there is extensive quotation and reasoning from the authoritative sources of the tradition. With Ugye-Yulgok, this is much less the case; Yulgok is so sure of the rectitude of his position that he is even willing to say that if Chu Hsi had intended its contrary, Chu Hsi would have been wrong. He has gone through all the sources, grappled with their seeming differences, and seen with unshakable clarity how they must all fit together. For him a nondualistic understanding of *li* and *ki* is the absolute foundation of everything; this is the starting point, and matters such as the Four Beginnings and Seven Feelings, Tao mind and human mind,

xxxii   *Introduction to the Four-Seven Debate*

original nature and psychophysical nature—the area of moral discourse that invites dualism—should be treated as corollaries.

The Importance of the Four-Seven Debate

The Four-Seven Debate shaped a distinctive intellectual agenda and divided loyalties on the Korean peninsula for centuries. The minds that politically and socially influenced and shaped Chosŏn dynasty society were steeped in this discourse—with passionate engagement by some, perhaps mere tolerance by others, but in any case it was the emblematic learning of the elite. Therefore, it is fundamental for understanding premodern Korea. This applies not only to its intellectual history but more broadly as well, for one can hardly understand a society of high culture without grasping the kind of thought that engaged their minds.

The debate was also important for Neo-Confucian thought in general. Neo-Confucianism is both a philosophical system and a way of life. Drawing on the richness of the Buddhist and Taoist traditions as well as the Confucian values at its core, this tradition locates the concerns of human personal and social development within a cosmic framework. It is in fact an anthropocosmic vision, a metaphysics and cosmology profoundly animated by human moral concern. Its proudest achievement is elucidating an understanding of human perfection and imperfection that is tied into the structure of the cosmos, on the one hand, and eventuates in guidance for self-cultivation in daily life, on the other. Everything, including human beings, is finally integrated into the single, all-encompassing normative pattern of existence, the Tao; at the same time *ki*, the concrete stuff within which the Tao has its only reality, is enlisted not only as the agency by which the Tao is realized in concrete actuality, but also to explain deviance from the Tao. Thus are joined together the monistic metaphysical/cosmological discourse of the one Tao with the dualistic concepts that are the ordinary stock in trade of moralists. Whether one describes this system as a monistic dualism or a dualistic monism, the centrality of the tension created by the cosmic-moral synthesis is clear.

The Four-Seven Debate is perhaps the most searching examination of this tension ever carried out. The two personalities at the center of this centuries-long inquiry, T'oegye and Yulgok, almost ideally represent the polarities involved. T'oegye certainly respected the metaphysical/cosmic framework of Ch'eng-Chu thought, but his overriding concern was self-cultivation. He was keenly attuned to the nuance of Confucian moral discourse, and the dualistic note of something to be fostered, and something to be warned against, purveyed through an array of paired concepts (original nature/physical nature, Tao mind/human mind, Four Beginnings/Seven Feelings), was of decisive importance in his mind.

For Yulgok, the brilliant theoretician, such matters were of no less import, but understanding had to be built from the basics. To him, nothing is more basic than the fundamental understanding of *li* and *ki*, and the realms of metaphysics and cosmology elucidated in terms of these concepts are the prior framework grounding their application to the complex concepts of human psychological and moral life. His reasons for this approach, apart from the systematic bent of his kind of mind, are as imbued with Confucian moral concern as are T'oegye's, but on a somewhat different level. He repeatedly deplores the fact that T'oegye and Ugye are not really clear about "the Great Foundation." The first chapter of the *Doctrine of the Mean* had concluded its brief discussion of the equilibrium of the not-yet-aroused mind and its harmony in perfectly responsive activity on a cosmic note: "Equilibrium is the great foundation of the universe; harmony is its universal path." Whether cosmic or moral-psychological in context, *li* and *ki* constitute a single consistent discourse establishing the ultimate place of humans within the cosmos. If the dualistic tensions of the moral life are conceptualized in a way that would give them cosmic status or in a way that is inconsistent with the ultimate unity and harmony of the cosmos, the whole vision collapses.

T'oegye and Yulgok, then, share a profound commitment to a single anthropocosmic vision of life, but each one's intellectual demand is focused differently. They argue the matter in terms of precisely how one should understand the relationship of *li* and *ki*, and this debate explores the most fundamental structures and possibilities of the Ch'eng-Chu system insofar as it is woven in terms of this conceptualization. The ultimate question being explored here, however, clearly goes beyond the technical adequacy of these concepts; it involves the question of whether and how man can be understood as a being in full continuity with the natural world, while still doing full justice to the moral life, which is apparently the most distinctive human phenomenon.

When the question is put thus we can see the place of this debate in the broad context of world philosophical and religious traditions. Familiar Western traditions most often have explicated the moral life in terms of a spirit/matter, divinely based discontinuity between humans and other creatures. Modern Western attempts to locate man thoroughly within an evolutionary, materialistic universe have had difficulty in grounding morality or meaning at all, as is clearly reflected in the prevalence of themes of alienation and absurdity in twentieth-century thought. Various forms of Hinduism and Buddhism, however, have moved in the opposite direction, swallowing the phenomenal world entirely into consciousness. The distinctive East Asian approach viewed the universe as a single organic whole, a living physical continuum including humans and all other creatures in a harmonious unity. Neo-Confucians, as we have seen, benefited much from Buddhist sophistication regarding consciousness, but the traditional organismic assumptions about the universe formed the matrix for their metaphysics.

Of the several sorts of metaphysical systems we have mentioned, this organismic viewpoint so thoroughly explored by centuries of Neo-Confucians now looms large on the horizon of Western thought. Ethics, rendered, along with metaphysics, virtually impossible by materialistic assumptions, has been reinvigorated against the background of a new wave of ecologically focused thought. As we turn our minds to consider the meaning of human existence in continuity with the entire web of life on our planet, we are exploring a new variation of a paradigm that already has a rich history of high intellectual development. Direct borrowings are unlikely: the American Philosophical Association will probably not have debates concerning *li* and *ki* on its annual convention program in the year 2000. But the sophistication of this monistic dualism or dualistic monism can teach us much about the kinds of conceptualization germane to this paradigm; the kinds of problems that attend options and emphases in *li-ki* thought foreshadow questions that will await those who pursue an ecologically founded ethics as well.

The Four Seven Debate, then, is a window through which we can look with a varying focus. In the foreground, it shows us the distinctive terrain of Neo-Confucian thought on the Korean peninsula. In the middle ground, it discloses potentialities and tensions in the Neo-Confucian vision as elaborated by Chu Hsi. And in the distance, its assumptions about humans and the world and the complex questions it explores regarding human moral placement in a cosmic continuum delineate issues and questions that may well be prominent on the agenda for the century to come.

CHAPTER 1

T'oegye's Letter to Kobong

The paragraph excerpted here was an almost incidental part of a letter on other topics T'oegye wrote to Ki Taesŭng (Kobong) in 1559. In his emendation to Chŏng Chiun's Diagram of the Heavenly Mandate, T'oegye had said: "The Four Beginnings are the issuance of principle; the Seven Feelings are the issuance of material force." Hearing of Kobong's critical discussion of this, he proffers a modification, and with this began the written interchange that was to become the central landmark in Korean Neo-Confucian thought.

A1a Also, I have heard from scholar friends something of your discussion of my thesis regarding the Four Beginnings and Seven Feelings.[1] I was already dissatisfied myself with the imprecision of the wording, and, having gotten word of your helpful critique, I am even more aware of its error. So I have revised it to read: "The issuance of the Four Beginnings is purely a matter of principle and therefore involves nothing but good; the issuance of the Seven Feelings includes material force and therefore involves both good and evil." I am not sure whether or not this way of putting it is acceptable.

CHAPTER 2

Kobong's Letter to T'oegye
on the Four Beginnings–Seven Feelings Thesis

> *Kobong wrote this letter in the third month of 1559. It pre-*
> *sents his basic objections, introducing themes that become*
> *broadened and deepened in the course of the ensuing debate.*
> *This letter evoked T'oegye's first major attempt to enunciate his*
> *position.*

Tzu Ssu [in the first chapter of the *Doctrine of the Mean*] says: "When joy, anger, sorrow, and pleasure are not yet aroused, it is called equilibrium; when they have been aroused and are all **A1b** perfectly measured, it is called harmony." Mencius says: "The sense of commiseration is the beginning of humanity; the sense of shame and dislike [for evil] is the beginning of righteousness; the sense of yielding and deference is the beginning of propriety; the sense of right and wrong is the beginning of wisdom."[1] As for these propositions regarding the nature and the feelings, the pronouncements of former Confucians have been perfectly clear. As I have understood it, Tzu Ssu was speaking of them in a way described as "speaking of them in their entirety," while Mencius's discussion is described as "singling out [the good side]."[2] For before a person's mind-and-heart is aroused, the condition is considered the nature, and after it is aroused, it is considered the feelings. In that case, the nature involves nothing but good, while the feelings involve both good and evil.

> *The nature-feelings relationship is cast in the pattern of the*
> *latent and manifest, which is frequently encountered in East*

3

*Asian thought; the Neo-Confucians spoke of this kind of relation-
ship as one of "substance and function." In this case, the nature
is substance, the latent, quiet condition of something just being
as it is. Feelings are function, an active condition that manifests
the pattern latent in the nature. Humanity, for example, is a
fundamental pattern or structure inherent to our nature; although it can never be directly observed in itself, this pattern is
manifest in the active life of the feelings as warmth, affection,
benevolence, compassion, and so on.*

*The nature, substance, is equated with li, and hence is per-
fectly good. Mencius's famous discussion of the Four Beginnings
(humanity, righteousness, propriety, and wisdom) was part of
his argument that human nature is good, so he is characterized
as "singling out" just those feelings that are a direct and pure
manifestation of the (good) nature. The comments about joy, anger, sorrow, and pleasure attributed to Tzu Ssu as the imputed
author of the* Doctrine of the Mean, *however, specify "when
they have been aroused and are all perfectly measured," that is,
the possibility of their being somehow excessive or deficient is
implied; thus he is said to speak of the feelings "in their entirety," including both good and evil. Although he mentions only
four such feelings, he is considered to speak for the whole body
of ordinary feelings symbolized by the conventional list of seven
found in the* Book of Rites.[3] *Kobong's contention, as we shall
see, is that the Four Beginnings are thus simply a subset of these
"Seven Feelings."*

Such is the definite rationale of this matter. It's just that in the
case of Tzu Ssu and Mencius, that with respect to which they were
speaking was not the same, and so there is the distinction between
the Four Beginnings [of which Mencius spoke] and the Seven
Feelings [of which Tzu Ssu spoke]. It is not that apart from the
Seven Feelings there are also the Four Beginnings. Now, if one
regards the Four Beginnings as being issued by principle and
[hence] as nothing but good, and the Seven Feelings as issued by
material force and so involving both good and evil,[4] then this splits
up principle and material force and makes them two [distinct]
things. It would mean that the Seven Feelings do not emerge from
the nature and the Four Beginnings do not mount on material force
[to issue]. What such wording conveys cannot but be considered

A2a problematic, and later students of the matter will certainly have doubts about it.

> *The nature, as* li, *is the formative, structuring element, while material force,* ki, *is the concretizing and energizing component of existence. Any activity therefore must involve both. What introduces a problem here is the Neo-Confucian use of "the turbidity" of* ki *to explain how distortion enters the picture. In its concretization and actualization through imperfect, turbid* ki, *the pure goodness of the original nature can become distorted, that is, evil. Such is not the case in the feelings spoken of by Mencius, but the potentiality is clearly there in the feelings spoken of by Tzu Ssu. T'oegye's initial formulation of a distinction between these feelings concentrates on the pure goodness of* li *in the case of the former and the possible disruption by* ki *in the latter, but as Kobong here objects, this does not seem to give due weight to the mutuality of* li *and* ki *in the arising of all feelings.*

And then again, if you amend it by saying, "The issuance of the Four Beginnings is purely a matter of principle and therefore involves nothing but good; the issuance of the Seven Feelings includes material force and therefore involves both good and evil" [cf. A1b], although it may be somewhat better than the former, in my view it likewise seems questionable. For if in the issuance of the nature material force does not interfere the original goodness [of the nature] can be directly manifested, and this is truly what Mencius described as the Four Beginnings. These are definitely purely a matter of that which heavenly principle issues. Nonetheless, they cannot emerge as something apart from the Seven Feelings; rather they represent the systematic sprouts (*myo maek*, Chin. *miao-mai*) of those among the Seven Feelings that issue and are perfectly measured.

So could it be permissible to take the Four Beginnings and Seven Feelings as mutually contrasting expressions and speak of them as [respectively] "pure principle" and "including material force"? In discussing the human mind and the Tao mind, perhaps one may use such an explanation, but when it comes to the Four

Beginnings and the Seven Feelings, I suspect one may not explain it in such fashion,[5] for the Seven Feelings cannot be seen exclusively as a matter of the human mind.

Principle is the master of material force, and material force supplies the material for principle. The two are certainly distinct, but when it comes to their presence in actual things, they are certainly mixed together and cannot be split apart. It's just that princi-
A2b   ple is weak while material force is strong; principle has no concrete sign, but material force is physically in evidence. Therefore when it comes to the matter of [concrete] activity and manifestation, there cannot but be divergences of excess or deficiency [because of the imperfection of material force]. This is the reason that in the issuance of the Seven Feelings, some are good and some evil, and the original substance of the nature at times cannot be integrally [manifest]. Nonetheless, [those of the Seven Feelings] that are good are the original condition of the Heavenly Mandate, while those that are evil are a matter of excess or deficiency in the psychophysical endowment of material force. This is what I describe as the Four Beginnings and Seven Feelings from the start not meaning two different things.

Recent scholars have not discerned Mencius's intent in approaching just the good side and singling it out and referring to it, so for the most part they discuss the Four Beginnings and Seven Feelings as differentiated from one another. In my humble opinion, that is a mistake. Master Chu says: "Joy, anger, sorrow, and pleasure are feelings. The condition before they have issued is the nature."[6] And then when it comes to discussing the relationship between the nature and the feelings, he time after time speaks of it in terms of the four characteristics of the nature [i.e., humanity, righteousness, propriety, and wisdom] and the Four Beginnings, for he feared people would not understand and would speak of the nature in terms of material force. Nonetheless, those who pursue learning must understand that principle is not external to material force, and cases where material force has its natural manifestation without excess or deficiency are the same as the original substance of principle. If they understand that and apply their effort in that direction, then perhaps they will not be much off the mark.

CHAPTER 3

*T'oegye's Reply to Kobong Arguing the Distinction
of the Four Beginnings and Seven Feelings in Terms
of Principle and Material Force*

> *In the eleventh month of 1560, T'oegye responded to Kobong's
> critique with this letter. According to his remark in the twelfth
> section of the letter, the long gap between Kobong's critique and
> this response owed to his own doubts about his position. He
> became convinced, however, when he found a passage in Chu
> Hsi's Yü-lei (Recorded Conversations) in almost exactly the
> same words he had originally used. Thus encouraged, he com-
> posed this letter defending his position; after receiving Kobong's
> lengthy critique of this letter, he rewrote it, changing the word-
> ing of certain passages in the light of Kobong's response (cf.
> below, A29a–33a). In his comments, Kobong divided T'oegye's
> letter into twelve sections. These divisions have been introduced
> into the text for ease of reference.*

A3a   Section One

As for the argumentation regarding the nature and the feelings, the pronouncements and clarifications of former Confucians
have been precise. But when it comes to speaking of the Four
Beginnings and the Seven Feelings, they only lump them together
as "feelings"; I have not yet seen an explanation that differentiates
them in terms of principle and material force.

[cf. Kobong's response, A7a–10b]

Section Two

Some years ago, when Mr. Chŏng made his diagram, it included the thesis that the Four Beginnings issue from principle and the Seven Feelings issue from material force. My opinion was that the dichotomy was too stark and would lead to controversy. Therefore, I emended it [in my letter to you] with the expressions "pure goodness," "combined with material force," and so on. This was for mutual support in working it out clearly. It's not that I thought there was no problem in the expression.

[cf. Kobong's response, A10b–11a]

Section Three

Now that I have received your critique pointing out my mistakes, my eyes have been opened, and I have benefited greatly from the warning. Nonetheless, there are still some elements that are not fully settled in my mind. Let me present my ideas so that you can help me get it straightened out.

Section Four

Indeed, the Four Beginnings are feelings, and the Seven Feelings are also feelings. Both are equally feelings, so why is there the distinct terminology of the Four and the Seven? What your letter describes as "that with respect to which one speaks" (*so ch'ui i ŏn chi*) being not the same is the reason. For principle and

A3b   material force are fundamentally mutually necessary as substance and are interdependent as function; there definitely can never be principle without material force or material force without principle. Nevertheless, if that with respect to which one speaks [in using such terminology] is not the same, then it is also true that it is not countenanced to not distinguish them. From ancient times, sages and wise men have discussed them as two; how has it ever been necessary to fuse them together as a single thing and avoid speaking of them as distinct?

[cf. Kobong's response, A11b–12b]

Section Five

And if we were to discuss the matter in terms of just the single word, "nature," Tzu Ssu refers to the nature that is the "Heavenly Mandate," and Mencius refers to the nature that is the "good nature";[1] to what, may we ask, does the word "nature" refer in these two cases? Could it be anything other than a matter of approaching the composite of principle as endowed with material force and pointing to this as the aspect of principle in its original condition as endowed by Heaven? Since the point of reference is principle, not material force, it therefore can be described as purely good and without evil, that is all. If, because principle and material force are inseparable, one therefore wanted to include material force in the explanation, then it would already be other than the nature's original condition.

> *This is a clear example of the thinking that led neo-Confucian thinkers to develop the idea of a perfectly good "original nature" conceptually but not existentially distinct from the imperfect "physical nature," that is, the nature as concretized in material force. Although the distinction is a conceptual one and all agreed that there are not two natures, Neo-Confucians would not readily say that the physical nature is the reality and the original nature represents a simple conceptual abstraction. T'oegye's side of the debate, in fact, could be viewed as a search for the consequences of the original nature in the phenomenal realm of the life of the feelings.*

Indeed, Tzu Ssu and Mencius had a penetrating view of the substance of the Tao in its integral wholeness and set up their propositions from that point of view, but that does not mean that they were aware of just the one side and not the other. It is really

because if one speaks of the nature as mixed with material force,
A4a   then one cannot see the original goodness of the nature. It was
only in later times, after the appearance of the Ch'eng brothers,
Chang Tsai, and other thinkers that a thesis regarding the physical
nature finally became unavoidable. That likewise was not just a
case of creating differences out of a fondness for complexity.
Since what they were referring to had to do with the condition
after having been endowed [with material force] and being born,
then it was also not practicable to refer to it without distinguishing
it from the original nature.

Therefore I recklessly venture that the distinction of the Four
Beginnings and Seven Feelings in the case of the feelings is similar to the difference between the original nature and the physical
nature in the case of the nature. If that is so, since it is considered
permissable to distinguish between principle and material force in
speaking of the nature, why should it suddenly become impermissible to distinguish between principle and material force when it
comes to speaking of the feelings?

[cf. Kobong's response, A13a–14a]

Section Six

From whence do the feelings of commiseration, shame and
dislike [for evil], yielding and deference, and right and wrong issue? They issue from the nature that is composed of humanity,
righteousness, propriety, and wisdom. And from whence do feelings of joy, anger, sorrow, fear, love, hatred, and desire issue?
They are occasioned by circumstantial conditions when external
things contact one's form and cause a movement internally. As for
the issuance of the Four Beginnings, since Mencius has already
referred to them in terms of the mind-and-heart,[2] and since the
mind-and-heart is the combination of principle and material force,
then why do we say that what is referred to in speaking of them
has principle as its predominant factor (*so chu*)?[3] That is because
the nature composed of humanity, righteousness, propriety, and

A4b   wisdom exists in its pure condition within us, and these four are the commencements [of its active manifestation]. As for the issuance of the Seven Feelings, Master Chu says they originally have a standard of what they ought to be, so it's not that they are without principle.[4]

But then why is what is referred to in speaking of them a matter of material force? When external things arrive, that which is most susceptible to stimulus and the first to move is our physical form, and the Seven Feelings are its systematic outgrowth. It does not make sense to say that [the Four Beginnings] are within us as pure principle, but at the moment they issue they are mixed with material force, or that what is externally aroused [i.e., the Seven Feelings] is physical form, but its issuance is the original substance of principle.

The Four Beginnings are all good. Therefore it is said, "Without these four dispositions, one is no longer human."[5] And it is also said, "As for the feelings, it is possible for them to be good."[6] In the case of the Seven Feelings, then, good and evil are not yet fixed. Therefore, as soon as we have them but are not able to exercise discernment, the mind-and-heart will not attain its proper condition. And only after they have issued with proper measure can they be called harmonious.

From this perspective, although neither of the two is separable from principle and material force, on the basis of their point of origin, each points to a predominant factor and emphasis, so there is no reason why we cannot say that the one is a matter of principle and the other a matter of material force.

[cf. Kobong's response, A14a–18b]

A5a   **Section Seven**

I have carefully examined your letter. You have profound insight into the interdependence and inseparability of principle and material force, and are very forceful in advocating this kind of explanation. Therefore, you look to the fact that there has never been material force without principle or principle without material force, and say that the Four Beginnings and Seven Feelings do not mean something different. Although this is almost correct, if you compare it with what the sages and worthies meant, I fear that there is still some discrepancy.

[cf. Kobong's response, A18b–19a]

Section Eight

In general, the study of moral principle is a matter of extreme subtlety and precision, so one must approach it with a greatness of mind-and-heart and a heightened scope of vision. It is absolutely wrong to enter into it with a preconceived emphasis on a particular thesis; rather, the main thing is to empty one's mind and approach it with an even attitude to see where the meaning leads. Approaching what is the same, one understands that it may involve differences, and approaching what is different, one sees that it may involve sameness. Distinguishing things as two does not necessarily prevent their never being separated, and when they are combined as a unity, it may actually come down to their not being admixed with one another. This is the all-encompassing approach that avoids one-sidedness.

Section Nine

I beg leave to go over the matter using the words of the sages and worthies in order to make clear the necessary truth of what I have been saying.

In antiquity, Confucius had the theory that the continuation [of the Tao in one's own person] is good and that which fulfills [the Tao] is the nature,[7] and Master Chou [Tun-i] had the thesis regarding the Indeterminate and the Supreme Ultimate. Both of these approach the interdependent pair, principle and material force, and single out and speak exclusively of principle.

A5b   Confucius spoke of the nature by which [humans are born] similar to one another [but become] dissimilar, and Mencius spoke of the nature with respect to the ears, eyes, mouth, and nose.[8] This is all a matter of approaching principle and material force in their mutual fulfillment of each other, and one-sidedly referring exclusively to the material force aspect. How are these four cases anything but a matter of approaching what is similar and understanding that there are also differences.

In Tzu Ssu's discussion of equilibrium and harmony [in the first chapter of the *Doctrine of the Mean*], he mentioned pleasure, anger, sorrow, and joy, but he did not mention the Four Beginnings. In Master Ch'eng's discussion on [Yen Hui's] Love of Learning, he mentioned pleasure, anger, sorrow, fear, love, dislike, and desire, but he too did not mention the Four Beginnings.[9] These approach principle and material force in their interdependence and speak without discriminating between them. Are not these two cases a matter of approaching what is different and seeing that there are similarities?

[cf. Kobong's response, A19a–20a]

Section Ten

But now your approach to the argument is quite different from this: you like sameness and hate difference; you take pleasure in the undifferentiated whole and dislike analytical distinctions. You do not seek the point of origin of the Four Beginnings and Seven Feelings, but generalize in terms of their combining principle and material force and including both good and evil, with a strong conviction that speaking of them in a differential mode is impermissible. In the course of your argument, although you say that principle is weak and material force strong, that principle has no concrete sign but material force is physically in evidence, when it comes to the conclusion, you regard the natural manifestation of material force as the fundamental substance of principle [cf. A2b]. If one follows this line of thought, it leads to thinking of principle and material force as one thing with nothing that distinguishes them. Recently Lo Cheng-an [Chin-shun, 1465–1547] has advocated the thesis that principle and material force are not two things

A6a

and has gone so far as to consider Master Chu's explanation as wrong.[10] Being a common sort of person, I have not yet been able to understand what he is getting at, which is not to say that the intent of your letter seems similar.

[cf. Kobong's response A20a–21a]

Section Eleven

And after your letter has already said that that with respect to which Tzu Ssu and Mencius speak is not the same, and further that you consider the Four Beginnings as singled out, then on the contrary you say that the Four Beginnings and Seven Feelings have no different referent [cf. A2b]. Is this not close to contradicting oneself?

Indeed, pursuing learning while disliking distinctions and concentrating on explanations that fit everything into a unity was characterized by the ancients as "a hawk gobbling dates whole"; this approach is highly problematic. And if one goes on like this, without even being aware of it, one may ineluctably slip into the abuse of discussing the nature in terms of material force and fall into the calamity of thinking of human desires as heavenly principle. How could this be allowed!

[cf. Kobong's response, A21a–22b]

Section Twelve

When I received your letter, I wanted to express my thoughts, foolish though they are, but I could not venture to view my opinion as necessarily correct and beyond question, and so for a long time I have not put it forth. But recently [I have found] a passage

A6b in the *Chu Tzu yü-lei*, the last section of his discussion of Mencius's Four Beginnings, that directly discusses this matter. His explanation is as follows: "The Four Beginnings, these are the issuance of principle; the Seven Feelings, these are the issuance of material force."[11] Have not the ancients said, "Do not venture to confide in yourself, but confide in your teacher!" Master Chu is the one I regard as my teacher, and he likewise has been revered as teacher by ages past and present throughout the world. Having obtained his explanation, I can finally have confidence that my own ignorant opinion did not involve any great misunderstanding; and Chŏng [Chiun]'s initial explanation likewise had no problem and seems not to need revision.

And so I have ventured to give this rough description of my notions in order to request your instruction on the matter. What do you think? If it seems that although the thrust is as stated, when it comes to the verbal expression there might be an imprecision that departs from the truth, then would it not be better to use the old explanations of former Confucians? If so, I suggest that we substitute Master Chu's original explanation and remove ours; then everything would be proper. What do you think?

[cf. Kobong's response, A21b–22b]

CHAPTER 4

*Kobong's Response to T'oegye's Letter Discussing
the Four Beginnings and Seven Feelings*

> *Kobong responded to T'oegye's letter with a forty-one-page, de-
> tailed critique. After a few preliminary formalities, he begins
> with remarks ostensibly addressed to Section One of T'oegye's
> letter, though in fact his remarks (A7a–10a) constitute a general
> introduction to his critique. He first seeks to ensure common
> ground by citing clear passages from Chu Hsi defining the na-
> ture and relationship of the mind, nature, and feelings. Then he
> mounts a preliminary attack on Section Six of T'oegye's letter,
> which he regards as the heart of the matter. With this, he turns
> to Section Two of T'oegye's letter and commences his more sys-
> tematic, section-by-section analysis, in which Section Six in its
> turn receives extensive further comment.*

On the First Section

A7a   I would say that as for the explanation of the nature and the
feelings, the discussions of the former Confucians certainly could
hardly be improved. Nevertheless, it is also the case that some are
precise and some are summary, and so they could not be exactly
alike. This means that what remains for us later scholars is just to
take fully into account the precise or summary character of their
discussions and repeatedly reflect on and thoroughly investigate
the matter in order to seek out what we may personally attain in
our own minds. This is permissible. What is impermissible is to

17

A7b   just depend on the explanations already formulated and summarily lump them together and say that the truth of the matter is like this and nothing more. Master Chu said:

> As for the distinction of the mind, the nature, and the feelings, with the Ch'engs and Master Chang [Tsai] it was fixed and uniform. But when it came to the various disciples of the Ch'engs, on the contrary what each understood as the fully formed explanation conveyed by their master consistently diverged.[1]

Indeed, if even what the Ch'engs' disciples understood as their master's explanation still could not avoid divergence, then how much more will such be the case with us later scholars!

Carefully thinking over the matter at issue, I feel that although in its broad outline there is nothing that amounts to a real obstacle, among the fine points there are a number that are still dubious; I fear that it cannot yet be considered as free from slight deviations [from what is correct].

Master Chu says: "As for the fact that the various Confucians' discussions of the nature are not the same, it's not that there is a lack of clarity regarding good and evil, but because the meaning of the word 'nature' is not unambiguously determined."[2] In my opinion, this is also the case with the question at hand: it's not that there is a lack of clarity regarding principle and material force, but I suspect that the words "mind" and "nature" and "feelings" have not been unambiguously determined, and that's the problem.

I would suggest, in the *Yü-lei* one passage says:

> As soon as the nature activates, then it is the feelings. The feelings have both good and evil, but as for the nature, it is entirely
>
> **A8a**   good. And the mind is that which embraces the nature and the feelings.[3]

Another passage says:

> As for the nature, feelings, and mind, Mencius and Heng-ch'u [Chang Tsai] have explained them well: Humanity is the nature, compassion is [the correlative] feeling that must be manifested in

the mind. The mind is that which governs and unites the nature and the feelings. The nature is just how something should be. It is just this principle, it's not that there is some actual matter there; if it were some actual matter then there being good, there would also have to be evil. It's only that it does not have some actual matter but just its principle, therefore it is nothing but good.[4]

And another passage says:

The nature is nothing but good. As for what the mind issues as feelings, sometimes they are not good. To say that what is not good does not pertain to the mind also will not do. This rather is a matter of the mind's fundamental substance originally being nothing but good; its slipping into what is not good is a matter of the feelings' being led astray by things and so that happens. "Nature" is the comprehensive term for principle; "humanity," "rightness," "propriety," and "wisdom" are all the terms for individual principles within the nature. "Commiseration," "shame and dislike [for evil]," "declining and deference," and "the sense of right and wrong" are the terms for what issues forth as feelings. They are cases where the feelings issue forth from the nature and are good.[5]

If one considers these three passages, then ones can mostly understand the words "mind," "nature," and "feelings."

[T'oegye agrees with these three quotations, A34b]

As for an explanation that distinguishes between principle and material force in terms of the Four Beginnings and Seven Feelings, **A8b** before this I never saw one. Now I have received your letter quoting the words of the *Yü-lei* to that effect, so I see that former Confucians have spoken of it. It was just that with my narrow and coarse learning I had not yet seen it, that is all. Nevertheless, in what is stated as "The Four Beginnings, these are the issuance of principle; the Seven Feelings, these are the issuance of material force," I still suspect that there cannot but be some fine points [to be considered].[6]

Your letter regards the feeling's being distinguished as the
Four Beginnings and Seven Feelings as similar to the nature's having the differentiation of the original nature and the physical nature. These words are very appropriate; truly they and Master
Chu's words mutually clarify one another, and my own opinion
has never been otherwise. Nevertheless Master Chu has a saying:

> When one discusses the nature of Heaven and Earth, one speaks
> with exclusive reference to principle; when one discusses the
> physical nature, then one speaks in terms of principle mixed to-
> gether with material force.[7]

If one considers the matter in the light of this, the statement "The
Four Beginnings, these are the issuance of principle" is speaking
with exclusive reference to principle, and the statement "The
Seven Feelings, these are the issuance of material force" speaks in
terms of principle mixed together with material force. And this
means that [the statement that] "these are the issuance of principle"
certainly cannot be altered, while "these are the issuance of material force" is not a matter of exclusively referring to material force.

A9a This is what I meant when I said that there cannot but be some fine
points [to be considered].

[T'oegye disagrees, A38a]

In general, although there are quite a few points of agreement
between your letter and my opinion, there likewise are quite a few
points of difference. What's more, the points where we differ are
major items; if we are not able to agree on these, then there is no
need to discuss the points of similarity or difference or right or
wrong in the rest of the explanation. We must first have a clear
discernment and strong confidence regarding these items, and then
we will be able to take up the points of agreement and disagreement, right or wrong, in the rest of the explanation.

For, according to your letter, the Four Beginnings are the
issuance of the nature's [principles of] humanity, righteousness,
propriety, and wisdom. Therefore, although [the issuance] is a
matter of the combination of principle and material force, what is

referred to in speaking of them focuses on principle. As for the Seven Feelings, external things stimulate the [physical] form, and they are moved within and issue forth thus conditioned. Therefore, they are not without principle, but what is referred to in speaking of them consists in material force. Therefore, the Four Beginnings are within as pure principle and at the moment of issuance are not admixed with material force; the Seven Feelings are stimulated externally by physical form, and their issuance is not the original substance of principle; so that from whence the Four Beginnings and Seven Feelings come is not the same [cf. A4a]. These words are truly what you, sir, have attained yourself. Therefore, in the **A9b** whole treatise, although there are manifold and multiple leads on the matter, the main meaning is nothing other than this.[8]

As for my ignorant opinion, it differs from this. Man's feelings are but one, and what they are as feelings definitely combines principle and material force and has both good and evil. It's just that Mencius approached the wondrous combination of principle and material force and exclusively referred to what issues from principle as nothing but good; these are the Four Beginnings. Tzu Ssu approached the wondrous combination of principle and material force and spoke in an undifferentiated way, so the feelings [he described] definitely combine principle and material force and have both good and evil; these are the Seven Feelings. This truly is a matter of that with respect to which they were speaking being different.

Nevertheless, principle itself is present in the midst of what are called the Seven Feelings, even though they may involve material force; when they issue and are perfectly measured, they represent the nature that is the Heavenly Mandate and the original substance, and are the same reality with a different name as what Mencius called the Four Beginnings. When it comes to those that issue and are not perfectly measured, that is the doing of [imperfection in] the psychophysical endowment and selfish desires, so they do not recover the original condition of the nature. Therefore, this is really what I was getting at in my former explanation when I said that it was not that outside the Seven Feelings there were **A10a** another Four Beginnings, and again when I said that from the start the Four Beginnings and Seven Feelings never meant two different things [cf. A2b], this is what I meant.

[T'oegye disagrees, 42a]

If we pursue the matter in this light, then in saying that the Four Beginnings particularly focus on principle and the Seven Feelings particularly focus on material force [cf. A4b], although the broad outline is the same, there are also fine points in which we do not mean the same thing. Indeed, if on the basis of words as clear and concise as those of Master Chu, the views of scholars unavoidably involve points of difference and agreement, is this not what is referred to as "a hair's-breadth divergence"? But in that case, if one interprets Master Chu's words in terms of your opinion, the matter is straightforward and easy to understand, while if one would substantiate them in terms of my views, the matter becomes intricate and difficult to comprehend. What was said about a hair's-breadth divergence I truly suspect applies not to you, but to me. It's just that when I consider the matter in terms of the *Chung-yung chang-chü* and the *Huo wen* and in the light of Master Chu's lifelong teachings, it makes me suspect that it might be like this. I humbly beg that you think it over carefully.

> *Kobong again takes up the issue of Section Six below, A14a–18b. The essence of his view is that all feelings arise in the same way, so far as li and ki are concerned. The Four Beginnings refer not to special feelings that are a more direct manifestation of our nature, but simply to feelings that are an accurate and undistorted manifestation of our nature. Thus they are in fact no different than any other proper and good feelings; they amount to the Seven Feelings when the Seven Feelings are not distorted.*

On the Second Section

A10b   "The Four Beginnings issue from principle, the Seven Feelings issue from material force." These two phrases, which Master Chŏng expressed in his *Diagram*, truly do not differ from what Master Chu said; when they are understood aright, how could there be any problem? My former doubts about it were truly a matter of fearing that it would lead to problems for those who do not understand.

In a general discussion of the Four Beginnings and Seven Feelings, there is certainly nothing impermissible in saying that the Four issue from principle and the Seven issue from material force. But when it comes to making a diagram in which you take the Four Beginnings and locate them in principle's circle with the characterization, "issue from principle," and take the Seven Feelings and locate them in the circle of material force with the description, "issue from material force," although the fundamental requirements of making a diagram make it unavoidable, it seems that this positioning cannot help but make them appear too sharply separated.[9] If later scholars see it and, noting its clearly defined form, separate principle and material force and discuss each apart from the other, then will it not have grievously misled them?

[T'oegye disagrees, A42a]

After that, I received your letter that emended it by saying that "the issuance of the Four Beginnings is a matter of pure principle and therefore is nothing but good; the issuance of the Seven Feelings combines material force and therefore includes both good and evil." This seems much clearer than the earlier expressions, but, in my humble opinion, it is not yet quite satisfactory. For if one speaks of the Four Beginnings and Seven Feelings as a contrasting pair, and thus displays them in a diagram that describes the one as "nothing but good" and the other as "including both good and evil," then people will look at it and wonder whether there are two kinds of feelings. And even if they do not wonder about two kinds of feelings, they might suspect that among the feelings there are two kinds of good, one issuing from principle and another issuing from material force. In this respect, it is not yet suitable.

[T'oegye disagrees, A42b]

Thus what I formerly questioned had to do with this matter. Now when I carefully scrutinize your letter and reexamine the diagram's explanation, it seems that what is dubious goes beyond just this matter. That is, although I am not yet sure on which side of

A11a

the question the true rights and wrongs lie, what I questioned in the past—whether it would lead to problems for those who do not understand—was not just a concern brought about by overscrupulous consideration.

[Response to Section Three omitted][10]

A11b   On the Fourth Section

The Four Beginnings and Seven Feelings are certainly both equally feelings, and as for there being different terminology for them, is it not because that with respect to which one speaks is not the same? The intent of my former explanation was just this, and now your letter likewise considers it so. Nevertheless, as for the phrase "that with respect to which one speaks is not the same," if one interprets it in terms of my explanation, then there is no problem as regards there being basically a single kind of feelings, but with dissimilarities in the way of speaking of them. But if one **A12a**   examines the meaning [of the phrase] in terms of your letter, then the Four Beginnings and Seven Feelings each have their own point of origin, and it's not just that the way of speaking of them is dissimilar. This means that although we use the same expression, what you and I each mean by it is something different, and this cannot be disregarded.

[T'oegye responds, A43a]

What's more, [even in my opinion] the dissimilarity in what was said by Tzu Ssu and by Mencius is not just a matter of [different] words, but as for their intent likewise, each had a particular focus. I have seen a letter of Master Chu's, the "Reply to Ch'en Ch'i-chih," that says:

> The nature is the undifferentiated substance of the Supreme Ultimate; fundamentally it cannot be described by language. But in its midst the ten thousand principles are repleat, and the greatest

of the major guiding principles are four in number: thus they are named with the terms "humanity," "righteousness," "propriety," and "wisdom." The disciples of Confuciuis had never fully elaborated them, but finally with Mencius they were fully presented. For in the time of Confucius the principle that the nature is good was so clear that although the items involved were not exactly expressed the thesis of itself was sufficiently complete. But by the time of Mencius swarms of heretics had arisen and at times they regarded the nature as not good. Mencius feared that this principle was not sufficiently clear and thought about how to clarify it. If he just spoke in an undifferentiated way of the integral substance, then he worried that it would be like a scale without weights or a ruler without inches marked; it would in the

A12b   end not be sufficient to enlighten the world. Therefore he spoke of it as distinguished into four units and with that the theory of the Four Beginnings was established.[11]

[T'oegye agrees with quotation, A34b]

How is this not a matter of that with respect to which they spoke being different, and the intention of each likewise having its predominant element? For when Tzu Ssu discussed the characteristics of the nature and the feelings, he did so in terms of equilibrium and harmony, and when he mentioned joy and anger, sorrow and pleasure, these were cases of feelings combining principle and material force and including both good and evil; this was certainly speaking of them without differentiating—what I have described as "speaking of them in their entirety."[12] In clarifying the principle that the nature is good, Mencius spoke in terms of humanity, righteousness, propriety, and wisdom and mentioned [the correlated feelings of] commiseration, shame and dislike [for evil], yielding and deference, and a sense of right and wrong; this was just a matter of speaking only of feelings that are good, which I have described as "singling them out."[13]

When the sages and wise men of ancient times discussed principle and material force or the nature and the feelings, there certainly were times when they spoke of them as combined and times when they spoke of them as differentiated. Their intention likewise in each case had a predominant element (*so chu*), and it is up to the scholar to be subtle in discerning it, that is all.

> *At this point in the debate, the phrase here translated as "predominant element" (so chu) starts to become important. "Chu is ambiguous, since its meaning can shift in differing contexts from something that one makes the "main or controlling thing" (chu) to something that is the "main or controlling thing." Kobong's idea is that Mencius and Tzu Ssu were making different points, so naturally what each made the main center of attention was different. T'oegye, however, is concerned with the existential foundation for the distinction; without this, it becomes essentially verbal, which he is unwilling to accept. Consequently, although he likewise speaks at times of the matter of intent and focus of attention, his tendency is to see chu more in terms of existential condition than a state of mind. A similar ambiguity extends to the use of the term in the Yulgok-Ugye round of the debate as well. In this translation, chu is consistently rendered as "predominant," accompanied by "element," "factor," "thing," and so on, as may best suit the context. The intention throughout is to preserve as far as possible the ambiguity of the original text rather than bring out clearly what I understand to be the author's intention in a particular passage, for the ambiguity itself has played a significant role in the unfolding of this controversy.*

On the Fifth Section

A13a   The points you make in this section are all extremely subtle and finely drawn; how could I venture to discuss it further? Nevertheless, there remain aspects to be discussed that may advance us yet further. Master Chu says:

> Before there is any particular material force, there already is a particular nature; in the case of material force, there can be nonexistence, but the nature, on the contrary, is always there. Although it may at a given time be present in the midst of material force, nevertheless the material force is material force and the nature is the nature; they do not become mixed.[14]

And again he says:

> As for the nature that is the Heavenly Mandate, if it were not for the material endowment, it would have no place to reside. That being the case, since in man's material endowment there are differences of clearer and coarser, more one-sided and more proper, therefore when it comes to the properness of the Heavenly Mandate [i.e., the nature] there likewise are the differences between the shallower and the more profound, the liberal and illiberal. One must recognize that one cannot but also call this condition the nature.[15]

And again he says:

> As for cases where the Heavenly Mandate is described as the nature, this is the nature in its ultimately fundamental and original condition.[16]

[T'oegye accepts all these quotes, A34b]
And again he says:

> In the case of Mencius, he has singled out the nature and described it in its original condition. As for I- ch'uan [Ch'eng I], he included the physical endowment and says essentially they are inseparable.[17]

[T'oegye raises questions, A43b]
And again he says:"The thesis regarding the physical nature arose from the Ch'engs and Chang [Tsai]."[18]

Looking at these few paragraphs, I feel that what are called the "nature of Heaven and Earth" and the "physical nature" are extremely clear and that the differences and similarities in what is said by [Tzu] Ssu, Mencius, the Ch'engs, and Chang [Tsai] can be seen. And again Master Chu says:

A13b   That whereby Heaven and Earth produce creatures is principle; its [actually] producing the creatures is a matter of the vital and physical stuff [of the universe, i.e., material force]. Men and other creatures must receive this psychophysical endowment in

order to have concrete form, and principle being in its midst is
thereby called "the nature."¹⁹

This takes up the case of Heaven and Earth and men and other
creatures and applies the distinction of principle and material
force; this certainly does not pose any problem as regards each one
[i.e., principle and material force] being a single [distinct] thing.
But if one takes up the case of the nature for discussion, what is
called "the physical nature" is just this principle in the condition of
having descended into the midst of material force, that is all; it's
not that there is another separate nature.

If this is so, then when one discusses the nature and speaks of
the original nature and the physical nature, it is not the same as the
case of distinguishing principle and material force in the discussion
of Heaven and Earth and man and other creatures, in which [prin-
ciple and material force] each itself remains a single thing. For the
[same] single nature is spoken of differently depending on what it
is in [i.e., whether it is considered with or without the limitation of
the psychophysical endowment], that is all.

When it comes to discussing the feelings, they issue as feelings only after the original nature has descended into the psychophysical endowment. Therefore, they are characterized as combining principle and material force and having both good and evil,
and when they become actively manifest, as a matter of course,
there are those that issue from principle and likewise those that
issue from material force. But although there is nothing impermissible in distinguishing them in this way, if one is to make a
precise determination of the matter, then it likewise seems that
A14a   [this way of speaking] is not without problems. All the more is this
the case if one distinguishes the Four Beginnings and Seven Feelings in terms of principle and material force, for the Seven Feelings are not spoken of with exclusive reference to material force. I
especially feel that the details of this point are not yet satisfactory.

[T'oegye disagrees, A38b]

*Kobong raises a difficult point here; it reflects a tension inherent
in Chu Hsi's synthesis, which might be described as a "dualistic*

monism." On the monistic side, li *and* ki *are described as so perfectly complementary that they amount to almost two distinguishable aspects of a single entity,* li *describing the formative/ normative aspect and* ki *accounting for concreteness, particularity, and activity. Clearly, no real existence, including actually occurring feelings, can but combine both these aspects. On the dualistic side, in order to preserve the Mencian doctrine of a good human nature not only as an abstraction but as an existential basis for the practice of self-cultivation, there is the doctrine that even though "*li *is in the midst of* ki *as the nature," *li *and* ki *are never admixed. In the light of this, the "original nature" is real, not abstract, but at the same time it exists and functions only in conjunction with* ki. *Kobong interprets this to mean that* li *and* ki *each invariably plays their own distinctive roles in the arising of all feelings. When he says that one may speak loosely of feelings that issue from* li *and feelings that issue from* ki, *what he means is simply that good feelings manifest the purity of the nature, whereas evil or mixed feelings reflect the imperfections of* ki. *T'oegye will not settle for this because it seems to leave* ki *as the final controlling factor and leaves no existential role for the profoundly and normatively human feelings spoken of by Mencius.*

On the Sixth Section

I would suggest that these paragraphs superbly discuss what it is that makes the Four Beginnings and Seven Feelings as they are. Truly this is the most important part of the entire essay. However, since it draws too sharp a distinction between principle and material force, what it considers a matter of material force is no longer spoken of in terms of the mixture of principle and material force, but rather refers exclusively to material force. As a result, the thesis becomes overly one-sided.

[T'oegye agrees, A34a]

Now I beg your leave to discuss first the fact that the Seven Feelings are not exclusively a matter of material force; after that, we can try to comprehend the matter [looking at your text] line by line. The *Doctrine of the Mean* [chap. 1] remarks:

Before the feelings of pleasure, anger, sorrow, and joy are

A14b   aroused it is called equilibrium. When these feelings are aroused
and each and all attain perfect measure, it is called harmony.
Equilibrium is the great foundation of the world, and harmony
its universal path.

[Master Chu's] *Commentary*[20] says:

"Pleasure, anger, sorrow, and joy are feelings. The condition
before they are aroused is the nature. Since one's nature is not
leaning toward one side, it is called "equilibrium." When feelings are aroused and each and every one attains perfect measure
that is the proper condition of the feelings; since there is neither
excessiveness nor deviation, it is called "harmony." The "great
foundation" refers to the nature as conferred by Heaven. All the
world's principles derive from this; it is the substance of the
Way. The "universal path" refers to that which follows the nature, insofar as it is what all under heaven past and present follow; it is the function of the Way. This refers to the proper
character of the nature and the feelings in order to elucidate the
meaning of the statement [in this chapter] that we cannot (for a
moment) separate from the Way.

The *[Chung-yung] huo-wen* comments:

Actually the myriad principles are all inherent in the nature conferred by Heaven. Pleasure, anger, sorrow, and joy each has its
proper place. Before they are aroused, they reside within in an
undifferentiated manner. Since there is no one-sidedness or deviation, it is called "equilibrium." When they are aroused and assume their proper place, since there is no excessiveness or deviation, it is called "harmony." It is called "equilibrium" to signify
the proper character of the nature, the substance of the Way.
Since it embraces all the principles of Heaven and Earth and all
creatures, it is called "the great foundation of the world." It is
called "harmony" to manifest the proper condition of the feelings, the function of the Way. Since it is what people and things
past and present all follow, it is called "the universal path of the
world." Indeed, the nature conferred by Heaven is perfectly genuine and supremely good, and that which is inherent in the hu-
A15a   man mind-and-heart in terms of the completeness of its substance and function in all cases is originally like this. Sageliness
and stupidity neither add to nor subtract from this.[21]

In the *Chang-chü chi-chü*[22] there is a passage of Mr. Li Yen-p'ing.[23] that says:

> The condition before one is aroused is called "equilibrium." It is the nature. When [the feelings] are aroused and are perfectly measured, it is called "harmony." If they do not attain perfect measure, then there is disharmony. The difference between harmony and disharmony is perceived only after [the mind] is aroused; this is a matter of the feelings, not the nature. This is the reason Mencius says the nature is good and also says the feelings "can become good." This theory originated with Tzu Ssu.[24]

[T'oegye accepts quotations, 34b–35a]

In my humble opinion, if we thoroughly understand what is called the theory of the Seven Feelings from this perspective, then it is conclusive that it does not refer exclusively to material force. Furthermore, [Ch'eng] I-ch'uan's essay on "Yen Hui's Love of Learning," and Master Chu's treatise on "Activity and Tranquillity in the *Record of Music*"[25] tally well with the precept of the *Doctrine of the Mean*. Indeed, since Tzu Ssu transmitted and established the discourse to elucidate the proper character of the nature and the feelings, how could it involve any inadequacy? And since the discussions of Masters I-chuan, Yen-p'ing, and Hui-an [Chu Hsi] are all like this, then where is there room for later scholars [such as us] to come up with different ideas?

A15b   That being the case, as for the Seven Feelings, do they not combine principle and material force and involve both good and evil? And are not the Four Beginnings those of the Seven Feelings that are [in accord with] principle and are good? If this is so, then the desire to separate the Four Beginnings and the Seven Feelings as belonging respectively to principle and vital force without any interaction between them can well be said to be one-sided.

Your argument states: "Commiseration, shame and dislike . . . [issue from] the nature." [Cf. A4a]

My humble position is that the Four Beginnings certainly issue from the nature comprised of humanity, righteousness, propriety, and wisdom, but the Seven Feelings also issue from the nature comprised of humanity, righteousness, propriety, and wisdom.

Otherwise, why did Master Chu say that pleasure, anger, sorrow, and joy are feelings, and the state before they are aroused is the nature? Furthermore, why did he say that feelings are the issuance of the nature?

[T'oegye disagrees, A39b]

Your argument states: "Pleasure, anger, sorrow, and joy . . . emerge [occasioned by external circumstances]." [Cf. A4a]

My humble position is: The sentence "External things contact the form and cause a movement internally" comes from [Ch'eng I's] essay on "[Yen Hui's] Love of Learning." However, if we examine the original text, it says: "As the form has already been engendered, when external things touch the form they cause a movement internally. When there is an internal movement the Seven Feelings emerge."[26] When it says "cause a movement internally," and then says "there is an internal movement," it is referring to the arousing of the mind-and-heart. When the mind-and-heart is aroused, the desires of the nature emerge; these are what we call feelings. This being the case, when feelings appear externally, they may seem to be occasioned by circumstantial conditions, but in fact they issue from within.

A16a

[T'oegye concedes, A34a]

Your argument states: "As for the issuance of the Four Beginnings . . . [it is] the commencement [of the active manifestation of the nature]." [Cf. A4b]

My humble position is: Both the Four Beginnings and the Seven Feelings issue from the mind-and-heart. Since the mind-and-heart is a conjunction of principle and material force, feelings certainly combine both principle and material force. It is not the case that there is a particular distinctive kind of feelings that only issues from principle and not from material force. This point truly calls for one to distinguish the genuine from the false.

[T'oegye disagrees with the implications Kobong sees here, A39b]

Your argument states: "As for the issuance of the Seven Feelings . . . [it is the systematic outgrowth [of physical form]." [Cf. A4b]

My humble position is: *The Record of Music* states: "Humans are born quiet; this is the nature conferred by Heaven. When it is stirred by things and moves, these are the desires of the nature."[27]

Master Chu says, "The 'desires of the nature' are what we call feelings."[28] That being the case, 'feelings' being stirred by things and moving is a natural principle. For it is because there really is a given principle within that there is a match with the stimulus given externally; it's not that there is originally no such principle within, but upon the approach of an external thing, there is a fortuitous match and [the mind-and-heart] is aroused and moves.

Since this is so, I am afraid that the sentence "When external things approach, that which is most susceptible to stimulus and the first to move is our physical form" does not express [any unique **A16b** character of] the Seven Feelings. If we are to discuss the matter in terms of being aroused by things and then moving, the Four Beginnings are exactly the same. When the stimulus is a child about to fall into a well, then the principle of humanity automatically responds, and the disposition of commiseration is thereby formed. When the stimulus is passing by a shrine or the court, the principle of propriety automatically responds, and a disposition of reverence is thereby formed. In being aroused by things, these are no different from the Seven Feelings.

[T'oegye disagrees with Kobong's conclusions, A39b]

Your argument states: "It does not make sense to say that [the Seven Feelings] are within us . . . the original substance of principle." [Cf. A4b]

My humble position is: When it is within, it is definitely pure Heavenly Principle. However, at that time it can only be called the nature; it cannot be called the feelings. But the moment it is aroused, it becomes feelings, with the differentiation of harmonious and unharmonious. For in the not-yet-aroused state, it is exclusively principle, but when it is aroused, it mounts material force to become active. Master Chu's treatise "On Origination, Flourishing, Benefiting, and Firmness" states: "Origination, flourishing, benefiting, and firmness are nature; production, growth, harvest, and storage are the feelings."[29] And again he says: "Humanity, rightness, propriety, and wisdom are the nature; commiseration, shame and dislike [for evil], deference and compliance, and the sense of right and wrong are feelings."[30] Indeed, in his treating production, growth, harvest, and storage as feelings, we can see the fact of mounting on material force to be active, and so the Four Beginnings are likewise a matter of material force.

[T'oegye disagrees with Kobong's conclusions, A40b]

A17a It is also stated in Master Chu's answers to his students that commiseration is material force, but that whereby we are capable of commiserating in such a way is principle.[31] This statement is particularly clear, but it refers only to the case [of the feelings'] issuance when material force is compliant; it does not involve the element of error from the turbulence and confusion [because of imperfect material force].

In your letter, you characterize the Seven Feelings as arising from circumstantial conditions and being aroused by our physical form. I feel uneasy about these assertions. And I find your reference to [the Seven Feelings as] externally stimulated by physical form and so not the original substance of principle particularly unacceptable. In that case, the Seven Feelings would be something external to the nature, and Tzu Ssu's reference to them as harmonious would be wrong.

But there is something even more out of line: Mencius's feeling of joy to the extent that he could not fall asleep was indeed joy.[32] Shun's punishment of the four criminals was anger. Confucius's mourning cry was sorrow.[33] When Min-tzu, Tzu-lu, Jan-yu, and Tzu-kung were in attendance upon him and the Master was pleased, that was indeed pleasure.[34] How could these cases not be the original substance of principle? And if one examines the cases of ordinary people, there are also times when Heavenly Principle is manifest. For instance, when they see their parents and relatives, they spontaneously feel joyful; when they see death, mourning, sickness, and pain, they suddenly feel sad. How can this not be a matter of the original substance of principle? If these

A17b cases are all the effects of physical form, then physical form does not have anything to do with the nature or the feelings. Could that be possible?

[T'oegye responds, A43b]

Your argument states: "The Four Beginnings are all good . . .

it is possible [for the Seven Feelings] to be good." [Cf. A4b]

My humble opinion is: This is precisely what Master [Li] Yen-p'ing referred to when he said the Mencian theory originated from Tzu Ssu [cf. A15a].

Your argument states: "As for the Seven Feelings, good and evil [are not fixed] . . . [after they issue and are perfectly measured] they may be called harmonious." [Cf. A4b]

My humble opinion is: Master Ch'eng says, "Before pleasure, anger, sorrow, and joy are aroused, how could they not be good? After they are aroused and have attained perfect measure, in every respect they are nothing but good."[35] Therefore, the Four Beginnings are certainly all good, and the Seven Feelings are also all good. Only if they fail to attain due measure after they have been aroused will they lean toward one side and become evil. How could it be said that good and evil are not yet fixed?!

[T'oegye concedes, A34a]

Now if you say, "Good and evil are not yet determined," and further say, "If as soon as we have them but are not able to exercise discernment, the mind-and-heart will not attain its proper condition. And only after they have issued with proper measure can they be called harmonious," then the Seven Feelings are quite superfluous and useless. And what's more, when they have issued but not yet attained perfect measure, what are you going to term them?

[T'oegye disagrees, A44b]

A18a   And the words "as soon as we have them but are not able to exercise discernment" come from [Master Chu's] Commentary on the Great Learning, chapter 7; its meaning is that as for the four feelings—anger, fear, pleasure, and worry—they should just arise anew [each time]; they may not have a prior fixed place in the mind-and-heart. In the *[Ta hsüeh] huo wen* it says:

> Joy and anger, worry and fear are responses to stimuli. Beauty or filthiness, bending down or looking up are based upon things' physical endowments and are functions of the mind. How could there just be some that do not come out correctly?! Only in the occurrence of affairs, if there are matters that are not discerned, then as for the response to them, unavoidably sometimes there

will be mistakes and moreover times when one cannot but be carried away with them. Then as for joy and anger, worry and fear, there must first be a movement internally, and then there may be cases in which they do not attain their correct proportions, that is all.[36]

This is a matter that pertains to the rectification of the mind-and-heart; quoting it as evidence with regards to the Seven Feelings is a different matter.

[T'oegye disagrees, A45a]

Indeed, having repeatedly analyzed the explanations in your letter not only with respect to precision, but checking it against what the sages and worthies meant and finding such differences, then as for the statement "On the basis of their point of origin reference to each has its distinctive focus and emphasis," although there seems to be room for doubt, I suspect that in fact it is all inappropriate.

[T'oegye disagrees, 45b]

T'oegye and Kobong agree that a differing focus and emphasis are involved in the Four Beginnings and Seven Feelings, but Kobong clearly sees T'oegye's intent to root such difference in some kind of an existential difference, "their point of origin." This is the crux of their disagreement.

A18b   That being the case, then as for the statements that the Four Beginnings are a matter of principle and the Seven Feelings are a matter of material force, how can we just say that they involve nothing impermissible? All the more so since this argument is not just a matter of impermissible terminology, but rather, I suspect that with respect to the reality of the nature and the feelings and the practical application to preserving [one's inborn good dispositions] and exercising reflection [in activity], in all these respects it has impermissible [implications]. What do you think about it?

On the Seventh Section

I do not have any [special] insight; I just based myself on what was meant by former explanations to the effect that the Four

Beginnings mounted material force and the Seven Feelings proceed from the nature. And when you concede [on these grounds]
that I have insight into the interdependence and inseparability of
principle and material force, I certainly cannot live up to it, and
my meaning really is not centered on that aspect of things. In this
respect, I fear that your words have missed the mark.

As for my statement that the Four Beginnings and Seven
Feelings have, from the start, never meant two different things [cf.
A2b], my reasoning was that if one says the Four Beginnings are
the same reality with a different name as the Seven Feelings when
they issue forth and are perfectly measured, then if one pursues
A19a   them back to their root and origin, I believe that two different
things are not intended, that is all. How could I regard them as
originally with absolutely no difference of meaning! If I were to
characterize them as having absolutely no difference of meaning,
would that not be out of line with what was intended by the sages
and worthies?

[T'oegye disagrees with Kobong's implications, A41b]

On the Eighth Section

Everything you discuss in this section has to do with the essence of the proper approach to reading books and investigating
principle. How could I venture to do anything but accept it and
attentively follow it!

On the Ninth Section

Since these passages all are based on [the authority of] the
ancient explanations of former Confucians, they are certainly beyond criticism. But there was included a phrase "one-sidedly referring exclusively to the material force aspect" [A5b], which seems
to me not yet quite suitable. For if it is referred to as the nature,
then even though it may have descended into the psychophysical
endowment, one may not exclusively categorize it as material
force.

[T'oegye concedes, A34a]

A19b   I would suggest that as for the *Analects* passage "The Master said: Men by nature are similar; by practice they become dissimilar,"[37] [Master Chu's] annotation says: "This is what is characterized as speaking of the nature in terms of its being combined with the psychophysical endowment." Nonetheless, the nature is the master and combines with the psychophysical endowment. Mencius says:

> It is due to our nature that our mouths desire sweet taste, that our eyes desire beautiful colors, that our ears desire pleasant sounds, that our noses desire fragrant odors, our four limbs desire ease and comfort. But there is also fate. The superior man does not say they are man's nature.[38]

In the annotation, Master Ch'eng says: "The desires for these five things are [from] human nature, however, due to [one's own] allotment, it is not possible for one to have them all as one might wish; this is fate."[39]

However, in the *Collected Commentaries*, Master Chu says [regarding the passage in *Mencius*]: "The word 'nature' is said with reference to the psychophysical endowment; the word 'fate' is spoken as a combination of principle and material force."[40] On this basis, one might doubt [my objection to your phrase]. But then one must consider the passage in the *Yü-lei* that says:

> As for Mencius saying "[these desires are due to] the nature; but there is also fate," this "nature" is spoken of as combined with the psychophysical endowment [with its desires for] food and sex.[41]

This being the case, one can see that whenever the word "nature" is used, it does not one-sidedly refer to material force. So if you say, "one-sidedly referring exclusively to material force," I fear that it is not correct.

And your argument also states that Tzu Ssu's discussion of equilibrium and harmony was a matter of approaching principle and material force and speaking of them without discriminating between them; then as for the Seven Feelings, how can they not be a combination of principle and material force?

[T'oegye disagrees, A41b]

A20a   Since your letter has not been able to avoid such inconsistencies, I would ask that you carefully reexamine it.

On the Tenth Section

Liking sameness and hating differences, taking pleasure in the undifferentiated whole and disliking analytical distinctions are common problems for those of superficial learning. Nevertheless, my intention has certainly never been to be satisfied with only that; I also desire thoroughgoing analytical distinctions.

As for the point of origin of the Four Beginnings and Seven Feelings and their combining principle and material force and including both good and evil, and so forth, I have already discussed it in detail in the previous section. But as for my statement "The natural manifestation of material force is the fundamental substance of principle," something remains to be explained. For principle does not appear as a concrete phenomenon, but material force is physically in evidence, so the fundamental substance of principle is vast and indistinct, with no shape that can be seen; it can be experienced only in the active flow of material force. This is what was meant when Master Ch'eng said, "One who is good at observing must rather observe it in the already active condition."[42]

[T'oegye concedes, A34a]

In my explanation, from the beginning I distinguished principle and material force as each having their boundaries and not being mixed up together. Coming to my statement that "the natural manifestation of material force is the fundamental substance of principle," this is truly the aspect in which principle and material force separate and converge; it does not regard them as a single thing.

And [Master Chu's] *Collected Commentaries* annotates the "Master Standing over the River" chapter of the *Analects* by saying: "As for the transformations of Heaven and Earth the past re-

A20b

cedes and the future continues it without a moment's stopping: this is the fundamental substance of the Tao."[43] Is this not a matter of recognizing and apprehending [principle] on the level of material force? And again [another passage says], "Someone asked about the matter of principle being manifested within material force. Master Chu said, 'If yin and yang and the Five Agents are mixed together without losing their proper pattern and sequence, then that is principle. If material force does not congeal principle likewise lacks any place to which it can adhere.'"[44] That being the case, when the natural manifestation of material force is neither excessive nor deficient, is that not the fundamental substance of principle? And moreover, are not the cases of commiseration and shame and dislike [for evil] likewise the natural manifestation of material force? But that by which it is thus is principle, and therefore [these feelings] are characterized as issuing from principle, that is all.

Indeed, if one considers the Four Beginnings as issuing from principle and the Seven Feelings as issuing from material force, broadly speaking, there is certainly nothing incorrect. But when it comes to the ultimate analysis of what makes them thus, if one holds that the issuance of the Seven Feelings is not the fundamental substance of principle, and moreover that the natural manifestation of material force likewise is not the fundamental substance of principle, then as for what is called "the issuance of principle," where could it be seen? And as for what is called "the issuance of material force," it would be something quite apart from principle. Such is truly the fallacy of overdoing differential explanations of principle and material force; one must be aware of it.

As for the theories of Lo Cheng-an, I have not yet seen them so I do not know what they are, but on the basis of this single statement, he seems exceedingly mistaken. As for me, I certainly do not regard principle and material force as a single thing, nor do I say that they are not different things. My explanation from the first never had this meaning, nor did it contain any such expressions. I am really afraid that you see something in my thesis that is in disagreement with you, and immediately conclude that there is nothing acceptable in it and do not examine the matter further. If that is not the case, then how could you make such allegations? I beg that you once again explain the matter and correct me.

A21a

On the Eleventh Section

In the former essay I compiled to explain my humble opinions, at the time I regarded Tzu Ssu as approaching the feelings in terms of their combining both principle and material force and including both good and evil, thus speaking of them in an inclusive way; therefore I described him as speaking of them in their entirety. Mencius, in approaching the feelings, only takes up those that issue from principle and so are good; therefore I described him as singling them out. Nevertheless, both alike are a matter of feelings. And so, as for references to "Four Beginnings" and to "Seven Feelings," how are the differences anything but a matter of that with respect to which one speaks, but as for the actuality, there are not two sets of feelings involved. Thus I later repeated and tied it up by saying that the Four Beginnings and Seven Feelings from the start have not meant two different things, and I was not aware of contradicting myself. Now after receiving your kind instruction, I again thought it through thoroughly and still do not see that I have [contradicted myself]. But how is this anything but the result of my being poor at self-knowledge!

As for discussing the nature in terms of material force, that likewise is not the intent of my explanation. If there is a problem of confusing human desires with heavenly principle, deep self-reflection and self-restraint are called for, that is all.

On the Twelfth Section

Master Chu certainly has been revered as teacher by ages past and present throughout the world; it is true that we should respect what he says. But we must also give precise consideration to points of similarity and dissimilarity [in what he says]. With regard to the meaning of "not yet aroused" and "after aroused" in [the first chapter of] the *Doctrine of the Mean*, Master Chu once based [his interpretation] on Master Ch'eng's saying, "Whenever the mind is mentioned it refers to the aroused condition"; because he misunderstood the intention of the saying, he vigorously debated the matter with Nan-hsien [Chang Shih] and Hsi-shan [T'sai Yuan-ting] and only then did he come to a full realization of the truth. In his letter to the gentlemen of Hunan, he himself speaks of his mistake:

> As for Master Ch'eng's saying, "Whenever the mind is mentioned it refers to the after-aroused condition," this saying refers to the mind of the "innocent baby,"[45] and the phrase "whenever the mind is mentioned," was a mistake in his explanation. Therefore he himself also recognized that it was inappropriate and rectified it. Certainly one should not hold on to a saying he revised and completely doubt whether all (the other) explanations are mistaken; and on the other hand one must not just regard it as an inappropriate saying and not inquire into the particular aspect it was trying to point out.[46]

These words are perfectly impartial and clear and should be taken as a guide by later scholars. If so, then as for the "this is the issuance of principle . . . this is the issuance of material force" passage, if one were to consider and compare it with the whole context of the discussion, then the fine points of similarity and dissimilarity would become evident all by themselves.

I don't know: should later scholars follow sayings that are **A22b** furnished with full context and are complete and well rounded, or should they follow words spoken by chance on some occasion that may refer to only one side of the matter? In such a case, what to follow or disregard does not seem difficult to decide, but I am not sure. What is your opinion on the matter?

[T'oegye takes issue, A46a]

As for the symbolism and the categorical relationships and distinctions in the *Diagram of the Mandate of Heaven*, it would be hard to find another as full and complete as this. Nevertheless, if I might give my humble opinion, it seems to include several dubious points that should be reconsidered and determined exactly; after that, perhaps it may not disagree with the ancients. If perhaps you do not agree [regarding modifying the diagram], then it would do to accompany these items with an analytical explanation of their meaning in a discussion inserted into the explanatory text. One cannot just say that one is using the old explanation of former Confucians [i.e., Chu Hsi] and just leave it as vague as that, lest having already made a mistake oneself, one goes on to make others mistaken. What do you think?

Postscript

A23a   . . . I happened to be looking through the *Chu-Tzu ta-ch'üan* and I discovered a passage that discusses this matter with great clarity. His "Reply to Hu Kuang-chung" says:

> Master [Ch'eng] I-ch'uan says: "As Heaven and Earth accumulates the most subtle [material force], those who receive the most excellent of the stuff of the Five Agents are human beings. Genuineness and stillness characterize the state before he is aroused. His fivefold nature is complete; [its elements] are called humanity, rightness, propriety, wisdom, and good faith. His form is already produced; external things contact his form and cause movement within. His interior moves and the Seven Feelings emerge; they are called joy, anger, sorrow, pleasure, love, hatred, and desire. When feelings flame up and get out of hand the nature is harmed."[47] When I carefully consider and get the real taste of these words, I find that what they are getting at is no different than the explanation in the *Record of Music*. What he describes as stillness also refers to the time before one is aroused, that is all. At this time, what is preserved in the mind-and-heart is Heavenly in its undifferentiated mode. There is not yet any of the falseness of human desires; therefore [the *Record of Music*] says: "When the nature endowed by Heaven is stimulated by things and moves, at that [moment] right and wrong, the genuine and the false are differentiated."[48] That being the case, if it were not for the nature, there would be nothing to issue from; therefore it uses the expression, "the desires of the nature." There is no difference between the word "moves" [in this passage] and the word "issues" in the *Doctrine of the Mean*,
>
> **A23b**   and its right and wrong, the genuine and the false" are just decided according to there being measure or no measure, and being perfectly in accord with the measure or not being perfectly in accord with it [as described in the *Doctrine of the Mean*], that is all. This is just what your letter stated as, "it is truly necessary in

this matter to understand the genuine and the false." But it is necessary to have cultivation [devoted to the condition before the mind is aroused] in the course of daily life, and then one will be able to understand when actively dealing with affairs. But if one is directionless and completely without self-mastery, and only tries to do something about it after matters are already upon one, it will be too late and one will not be up to handling it correctly.[49]

And in his "Reply to Hu Po-feng" he says:

For when Mencius said that the nature is good, he was speaking in terms of its original substance, that is, the not yet aroused condition of humanity, righteousness, propriety, and wisdom. When he said "it can be good," he was speaking in terms of its aspect as function, that is the Four Beginnings, feelings that issue and are perfectly moderated. For in the matter of the nature and the feelings, although there is the difference between the not yet aroused condition and the already aroused condition, nevertheless that which he speaks of as "good" is the systematic connection that runs throughout everything, and in this there has never been any difference.[50]

Then he annotates this with the words of Master Ch'eng:

Joy and anger, sorrow and pleasure, as for the time before they have been aroused, when are they ever not good? When they issue and are perfectly measured, then there is no respect in which they are not good.[51]

A24a   If one considers the matter in the light of these two letters, then what we have argued thus far is not difficult to decide. I would imagine that you have certainly already seen [these letters], but I fear you may not yet have gone so far as to compare them [with our discussion], so I now include them in order to get your correction [of my understanding]. I am not sure what you will finally think of the matter.

I have observed that of late quite a few well-known and eminent men are pursuing this kind of study. Although their attainments differ with regard to the degree of profundity or super-ficiality and roughness or precision, in their discussions for the most part they follow the same rut. I suppose that is because the kind of sayings passed on in conventional circles naturally are of the same sort, like branches and leaves [of the same tree]. As for the explanation of the Four Beginnings and Seven Feelings, every time I heard my elders speak of it, they also categorized them according to principle and material force. To my mind, this was doubtful, and I wanted to question them about it, but considering my own fundamental lack of study, I did not venture to express myself lightly. Thus I have been silent and pent up about this for years. Now I have had the good fortune to meet you, sir, and have a chance to come out with my reckless words; although I cannot deny that I have been presumptuous, I also have finally almost rid myself of my [former] dense bewilderment. What good fortune!

A24b   I have thought about the matter, and my feeling is that the root of the difficulty of this generation in discussing the nature and the feelings goes back to Hu Yün-feng.[52] I would suggest that in his annotation to the fourth section of the first chapter of the *Great Learning* Mr. Hu says, "When the nature issues as feelings at first they are nothing but good; when the mind issues as the intention, then there is good and not good." These phrases were originally an interpretation of the words "that which it issues" in [Master Chu's] commentary [on this section].[53] And his expression is misleading insofar as it leads scholars to the further notion that the "feelings" are nothing but good and so belong with the Four Beginnings. Then that which is called the Seven Feelings does not belong any-where, and since they include what is not good, they seem to be the opposite of the Four Beginnings. Thus [these conventional scholars] go on to divide the way they speak of them and regard the Seven Feelings as the issuance of material force. How could this be [an accurate] understanding of what it means that the nature is nothing but good and as soon as the nature issues, it is the feelings and there is both good and evil! How could it be an [accu-rate] understanding of what Mencius meant when he said that "the feelings are able to be good,"[54] approaching just the good aspect and singling it out!

From this snarled confusion, they end up regarding each as

having its own separate point of origin (*so chongnae*);[55] how can this not be a mistake! Indeed, to say each has its own point of origin means that the source from which they issue is not the same. The Four Beginnings and the Seven Feelings both issue from the nature; could it be permissible to say that each has its own point of origin?! If one said those of the Four Beginnings and the Seven Feelings that are perfectly measured and those which are not perfectly measured each had their own point of origin, perhaps it would approximate the truth.

A25a

All these problems originated with Mr. Hu's mistake, and it is lamentable that later scholars have not been able to carefully consider and clearly discern the matter to find the most appropriate solution.

My outspokenness has gone so far that I have been exceedingly presumptuous and gone far beyond the bounds. Nevertheless, if you do not just consider my fault in speaking thus but rather give further precise examination to the matter, I suspect that it may have something of use.

And in Master Chu's *Diagram of the Nature*[56] he uses "the nature is good" to characterize the nature. Therefore, in his own annotations he says, "the nature is nothing but good." Below that in double columns, side by side, he puts "good" and "evil" to characterize the feelings. Therefore, under "good" he comments, "that which issues and is in perfect measure; there is no respect in which it is not good." And under "evil" he comments, "What is evil cannot be said to come directly from the good [i.e., the nature]; it's just that what is unable to be good leans to one side and becomes evil." This diagram appears in the twenty-ninth *chüan* of the *Hsing-li ta-ch'üan*, so you can examine it there.

A25b

Indeed, the view that the Four Beginnings are the issuance of principle and are nothing but good is originally based on the point of view from which Mencius was speaking of them. But if one considers feelings in general and exactly discusses them, then the issuance of the Four Beginnings likewise involves cases that are not perfectly measured; one certainly cannot say that in all cases they are good. If you take an ordinary, common person, sometimes he will feel shame and dislike for what he should not feel shame and dislike, and sometimes he will have a sense of right or wrong about what should not be judged right or wrong. For principle is in the midst of material force and mounts it in order to become actively manifest. Principle is weak and material force is strong, so when [principle's] control of it does not succeed when [material force] flows into activity, it is certainly easy for such cases to occur.

> *When Kobong observes that the Four Beginnings likewise go astray on occasion, what he means is that as feelings humanity, righteousness, propriety, and wisdom are no more impervious to excess and deficiency than are other feelings. This view is the logical consequence of his seeing the Four Beginnings as merely a subset of the Seven Feelings. As we shall see, he can still readily concede that Mencius discussed these dispositions with the intent of clarifying the inherent goodness of human nature; thus the fact that they can go astray is certainly not part of the meaning conveyed in the term "Four Beginnings."*

How then can it be that feelings have no evil, moreover, how can one regard the Four Beginnings as having no evil? This truly is a matter to which those who study should give an exacting examination. If one does not distinguish the genuine and the false, but just considers them as nothing but good, then the problem of taking human desires for Heavenly principle will certainly become indescribable. What do you think?

A26a   What I presented earlier all took the Four Beginnings as a matter of principle and as good; and now here I am speaking of the issuance of the Four Beginnings as also involving cases that may not be perfectly measured. These words seem to contradict each other, and I can imagine you might think it strange. Nevertheless, if such a way of expressing it is carefully thought through there is not necessarily any problem with its rationale and it can be fit into a single consistent explanation. I would be glad if we could take this up and think it out.

[The last six pages (26a–28b) of Kobong's postscript have been omitted][57]

CHAPTER 5

*T'oegye's Reply to Kobong's Critique of Distinguishing
the Four Beginnings and Seven Feelings in Terms
of Principle and Material Force, with a
Revised Version of His First Letter*

A29a   Having received the kind instruction of your second letter, I recognized that my words in my first letter were in some cases inexact or missed the mark. Therefore I have corrected it, and will first present the revised version to see if it is acceptable or not. After that, I have continued the discussion in a second letter, and I hope you will respond and clarify the matter for me.

[Revised Draft of T'oegye's First Letter]

> *At each point where he changed something, T'oegye inserted an interlinear annotation presenting the original text. In this translation, the same effect is achieved by striking over the changed wording and boldfacing the new wording.*

[Section One]¹

As for the argumentation regarding the nature and the feelings, the pronouncements and clarifications of former Confucians have been precise. But when it comes to speaking of the Four Beginnings and the Seven Feelings, they only lump them together as "feelings"; I have not yet seen an explanation that differentiates them in terms of principle and material force.

[Section Two]

Some years ago, when Mr. Chŏng made his diagram, it included the thesis that the Four Beginnings issue from principle and the Seven Feelings issue from material force. My opinion was that the dichotomy was too stark and would lead to controversy. Therefore, I emended it with the expressions "pure goodness," "combined with material force," and so on, for I wanted to support him in working it out clearly. It's not that I thought there was no problem in the expression.

[Section Three]

Now that I have received your critique pointing out my mistakes, my eyes have been opened, and I have benefited greatly from the warning. Nonetheless, there are still some elements that are not fully settled in my mind. Let me present my ideas so that you can help me straighten it out.

[Section Four]

Indeed, the Four Beginnings are feelings, and the Seven Feelings are also feelings. Both are equally feelings, so why is there the distinct terminology of the Four and the Seven? What your letter describes as "that with respect to which one speaks" being not the same is the reason. For principle and material force are fundamentally mutually necessary as substance and are interdependent as function; there definitely can never be principle without material force or material force without principle. Nevertheless, if that with respect to which one speaks [in using such terminology] is not the same, then it is also true that it is not countenanced not to distinguish them. From ancient times, sages have discussed them as two; how has it ever been necessary to fuse them together as a single thing and avoid speaking of them as distinct?

A29b

[Section Five]

And if we were to discuss the matter in terms of just the single word, "nature," Tzu Ssu refers to the "nature that is the Heavenly Mandate," and Mencius refers to as the "nature that is the good nature";[2] to what, we may ask, do these two uses of the word "nature" refer? Could it be anything other than a matter of approaching the composite of principle as endowed with material force and pointing to this as the aspect of principle in its original condition as endowed by Heaven? Since the point of reference is principle, not material force, it therefore can be described as purely good and without evil, that is all. If, because principle and material force are inseparable, one therefore wanted to include material force in the explanation, then it would already be other than the nature's original condition.

Indeed, Tzu Ssu and Mencius have a penetrating view of the substance of the Tao in its integral wholeness and set up their propositions from that point of view, but that does not mean that they are aware of just the one side and not the other. It is really because if one speaks of the nature as mixed with material force, then one cannot see the original goodness of the nature. It was only in later times, after the appearance of the Ch'eng brothers, Chang Tsai, and other thinkers, that a thesis regarding the physical nature finally became unavoidable. That likewise was not just a case of creating differences out of a fondness for complexity. Since what they were referring to had to do with the condition after having been endowed [with material force] and born, then it was also not practicable to refer to it ~~without distinguishing it from the original nature.~~ **purely in terms of the original nature**. Therefore, I recklessly ventured that the distinction of the Four Beginnings and Seven Feelings in the case of the feelings was similar to the difference between the original nature and the physical nature in the case of the nature. If that is so, since it is considered permissible to distinguish between principle and material force in speaking of the nature, why should it suddenly become impermissible to distinguish between principle and material force when it comes to speaking of the feelings?

A30a

[Section Six]

From whence do the feelings of commiseration, shame and dislike [for evil], yielding and deference, and right and wrong issue? They issue from the nature, which is composed of humanity, righteousness, propriety, and wisdom. And from whence do feelings of joy, anger, sorrow, fear, love, hatred, and desire issue? They are occasioned by circumstantial conditions when external things contact one's form and cause a movement internally. As for the issuance of the Four Beginnings, since Mencius has already referred to them in terms of the mind-and-heart,[3] and since the mind-and-heart is the combination of principle and material force, then why do we say that what is referred to in speaking of them has principle as its predominant factor (*so chu*)? That is because the nature composed of humanity, righteousness, propriety, and wisdom exists in its pure condition within us, and these four are the commencements [of its active manifestation]. As for the issuance of the Seven Feelings, ~~Master Chu says they originally have a standard of what they ought to be, so it's not that they are without principle.~~ **Master Ch'eng speaks of them as "a movement within," and Master Chu characterizes them as "each having its proper place," so they definitely likewise combine principle and material force.**

But then why is what is referred to in speaking of them a matter of material force? When external things arrive, that which is most susceptible to stimulus and the first to move is our physical form, and the Seven Feelings are its systematic outgrowth. It does not make sense to say that [the Four Beginnings] are within us as pure principle, but, at the moment they issue, they are mixed with material force, or that what is externally aroused [i.e., the Seven Feelings] is physical form, but its issuance ~~is the original substance of principle.~~**looks back to principle not to material force.**

The Four Beginnings are all good. Therefore, it is said, "Without these four dispositions, one is no longer human."[4] And it is also said, "As for the feelings, it is possible for them to be good." In the case of the Seven Feelings, then, ~~good and evil are~~

A30b

~~not yet fixed. Therefore as soon as we have them but are not able to exercise discernment, the mind and heart will not attain its proper condition. And only after they have issued with proper measure can they be called harmonious.~~they are originally good but easily devolve into evil. Therefore, when they issue with proper measure, they are called "harmonious." As soon as we have them but are not able to exercise discernment, then the mind-and-heart is already in the condition of missing its **A31a** proper condition. From this perspective, then, although neither of the two is separable from principle and material force, on the basis of their point of origin, each points to a predominant factor ~~and emphasis,~~ so there is no reason why we cannot say that the one is a matter of principle and the other a matter of material force.

[Section Seven]

I have carefully examined your letter. You have profound insight into the interdependence and inseparability of principle and material force, and are very forceful in advocating this kind of explanation. Therefore, you look to the fact that there has never been material force without principle or principle without material force, and say that the Four Beginnings and Seven Feelings do not mean something different. Although this is almost correct, if you compare it with what the sages and worthies meant, I fear that there is still some discrepancy.

[Section Eight]

In general, the study of moral principle is a matter of extreme subtlety and precision, so one must approach it with a greatness of mind-and-heart and a heightened scope of vision. It is absolutely wrong to enter into it with a preconceived emphasis on a particular thesis; rather, the main thing is to empty one's mind and approach it with an even attitude to see where the meaning leads. Approaching what is the same, one understands that it may involve differences, and approaching what is different, one sees that it may involve sameness. Distinguishing things as two does not necessarily prevent their never being separated, and when they are combined as a unity, it may actually come down to their not being admixed with one another. This is the all-encompassing approach that avoids one-sidedness.

[Section Nine]

A31b   I beg leave to go over the matter using the words of the sages and worthies in order to make clear the necessary truth of what I have been saying.

In antiquity, Confucius had the theory that the continuation [of the Tao in one's own person] is good and that which fulfills [the Tao] is the nature,[5] and Master Chou [Tun-i] had the thesis regarding the Indeterminate and the Supreme Ultimate. Both of these approach the interdependent pair, principle and material force, and single out and speak exclusively of principle. Confucius spoke of the nature by which [humans are born] similar to one another [but become] dissimilar, and Mencius spoke of the nature with respect to the ears, eyes, mouth, and nose.[6] This is all a matter of approaching principle and material force in their mutual fulfillment of each other and ~~one-sidedly referring exclusively to the material force aspect.~~ **referring to the combination, but with a predominant focus on material force.** How are these four cases anything but a matter of approaching what is similar and understanding that there are also differences?

In Tzu Ssu's discussion of equilibrium and harmony [in the first chapter of the *Doctrine of the Mean*], he mentioned pleasure, anger, sorrow, and joy, but he did not mention the Four Beginnings. In Master Ch'eng's discussion on [Yen Hui's] Love of Learning,[7] he mentioned pleasure, anger, sorrow, fear, love, dislike, and desire, but he too did not mention the Four Beginnings. These approach principle and material force in their interdependence and speak without discriminating between them. Are not these two cases a matter of approaching what is different and seeing that there are similarities?

[Section Ten]

But now your approach to the argument is quite different from this: you like sameness and hate difference; you take pleasure in the undifferentiated whole and dislike analytical distinctions. You do not seek the point of origin of the Four Beginnings and Seven Feelings but generalize in terms of their combining principle and material force and including both good and evil, with a strong conviction that speaking of them in a differential mode is impermissible. In the course of your argument, although you say that principle is weak and material force strong, that principle has no concrete sign but material force is physically in evidence, when it comes to the conclusion, you regard the natural manifestation of material force as the fundamental substance of principle. If one follows this line of thought it ~~leads to thinking of principle and material force as one thing with nothing that distinguishes them. Recently Lo Cheng an has advocated the thesis that principle and material force are not two things and has gone so far as to consider Master Chu's explanation as wrong. Being a common sort of person I have not yet been able to understand what he is getting at, which is not to say that the intent of your letter seems similar.~~ **seems the kind of thing that leads to thinking of principle and material force as one thing with nothing that distinguishes them. If you really consider them one thing with nothing that distinguishes them, I cannot claim that I can understand it. If that is not the case, and in the end you regard them as not a single thing and having some differentiation—therefore, putting the word "as" (yŏn) before "fundamental substance" [when you said "Cases in which material force has no excess or deficiency, but manifests naturally it is as the fundamental substance of principle"][8]—then why just in the case of a diagram do you regard as impermissible a mode of speaking that distinguishes them?**

A32a

[Section Eleven]

A32b

And after your letter has already said that that with respect to which Tzu Ssu and Mencius speak is not the same, and further that you consider the Four Beginnings as singled out, and then on the contrary you say that the Four Beginnings and Seven Feelings have no different referent, is this not close to contradicting oneself? Indeed, to pursue learning while disliking distinctions and concentrating on explanations that fit everything into a unity was characterized by the ancients as "a hawk gobbling dates whole"; this approach is highly problematic. And if one goes on like this, without even being aware of it, one may ineluctably slip into the abuse of discussing the nature in terms of material force and fall into the calamity of thinking of human desires as Heavenly principle. How could this be allowed!

[Section Twelve]

When I received your letter, I wanted to express my thoughts, foolish though they are, but I could not venture to view my opinion as necessarily correct and beyond question, and so for a long time I have not put it forth. But recently [I have found] a passage in the *Chu Tzu yü-lei*, the last section of his discussion of Mencius's Four Beginnings, that directly discusses this matter. His explanation is as follows: "The Four Beginnings, these are the issuance of principle; the Seven Feelings, these are the issuance of material force."[9] Have not the ancients said, "Do not venture to confide in yourself, but confide in your teacher"! Master Chu is the one I regard as my teacher, and likewise has been revered as teacher by ages past and present throughout the world. Having obtained his explanation, I can finally have confidence that my own ignorant opinion did not involve any great misunderstanding; and Chŏng [Chiun]'s initial explanation likewise had no problem and seems not to need revision. And so I have ventured to give this rough description of my notions in order to request your instruction on the matter. What do you think? If it seems that although the thrust is as stated, when it comes to the verbal expression, there might be an imprecision that departs from the truth, then would it not be better to use the old explanations of former Confucians? If so, I suggest that we substitute Master Chu's original explanation and remove ours; then everything would be proper. What do you think?

A33a

T'oegye's Second Letter Replying to Kobong's Critique of the Distinction of the Four Beginnings and Seven Feelings in Terms of Principle and Material Force

In this letter, after some appreciative introductory remarks, T'oegye categorizes points of agreement and disagreement with Kobong's complex critique. His itemization under the various categories has been indicated by bullets (•). He then proceeds with a detailed analysis of the seventeen points of partial or total disagreement.

A33b

A34a

. . . For there are cases where what you wrote is fundamentally correct, and I have been mistaken and erroneous in my discussion of the matter; there are cases where I have received your instruction and realized that my expressions missed the mark; there are cases in which what you instruct and what I have heard are fundamentally the same and do not differ; there are cases in which we are fundamentally the same but draw different conclusions; and there are cases where our views are different, and in the end I cannot accept what you say. I would list the items that belong to these five categories as follows:

- On the Tenth Section: The natural manifestation of material force is the original substance of principle.

This one item is a case of your words being fundamentally correct, and I was mistaken and my view erroneous; I have already revised it.

- On the Sixth Section: The thesis that the Seven Feelings are not exclusively a matter of material force.
- The same section: Your argument says that both kinds of feelings although they are [externally] conditioned in fact proceed from within.
- [The same section:] Your argument about good and evil being indeterminate in the case of the Seven Feelings.
- On the Ninth Section: On saying [the Seven Feelings] are a one-sided reference and exclusively refer to material force.

In the case of these four items, I have received your instruction and realized that my expression has missed the mark. I have also already revised them.

A34b
- On the First Section: The three items quoting passages from Master Chu's *Yü-lei* on the mind-and-heart, the nature, and the feelings.
- On the Fourth Section: The quote from Master Chu's letter replying to Ch'en Ch'i-chih that clarifies that that with respect to which one speaks is not the same.
- On the Fifth Section: the following quotes from Master Chu:
  The first item, explaining that the nature is not admixed with material force.
  The second item, explaining differences in the psychophysical endowment mean the Heavenly Mandate likewise is changed and that also one cannot say it is not the nature.
  The third item, that the nature that is the Heavenly Mandate is the ultimate, fundamental, absolutely original nature.
- On the Sixth Section: The quotes from:
  The *Chung-yung chang-chü*;

A35a
  The *Huo-wen*;
  Yen-p'ing [Li T'ung]'s explanation;
  all of which explain the Seven Feelings are a combination of both principle and material force.
  Master Ch'eng's essay "On [Yen Hui's] Love of Learning";
  Master Chu's explication of activity and tranquility [in the *Record of Music*].

The above thirteen items[10] are fundamentally the same as what I have heard and do not differ; they will not be discussed further.

- On the First Section: That the nature of Heaven and Earth is an exclusive reference to principle, while the physical nature is a matter of principle as admixed with material force; saying the one is the issuance of principle is definitely correct, but saying the other is the issuance of material force does not mean it is an exclusive reference to material force.
- On the Fifth Section: There is no problem with differentiating between principle and material force in speaking of Heaven and Earth or humans and other creatures, but discussing the nature is a matter of principle as descended into the midst of material force. If one discusses the feelings, then it is the nature as descended into the midst of the psychophysical endowment; they combine principle and material force and include both good and evil, so categorizing them differently [in terms of principle and material force] is questionable.

A35b
- On the Sixth Section:
   The first item of your argument, that the Seven Feelings likewise issue from humanity, righteousness, propriety, and wisdom.
   The third item of your argument, that it's not that there is a separate kind of feelings that only issue from principle and not from material force.
   The fourth item of your argument, that it's not that there is no [relevant] principle within and [the Seven Feelings] are aroused by a fortuitous stimulus by external things; that being stimulated by things and moving is likewise the case for the Four Beginnings.
   The fifth item of your argument, that as soon as they issue, they mount material force to be active, and so on; that the Four Beginnings are likewise a matter of material force.
- On the Seventh Section: That in pursuing them back to their root and origin, two different things are not intended.
- On the Ninth Section: That whenever the word "nature" is used, it does not one-sidedly refer to material force, and so on; that the Seven Feelings likewise are a combination of principle and material force.

Concerning the above eight items, our view is fundamentally the same, but we draw different conclusions.

A36a • On the First Section: That they are the same reality, but differently named; that it's not that apart from the Seven Feelings there are also the Four Beginnings; that the Four Beginnings and Seven Feelings do not mean different things.

• On the Second Section: That in a general discussion there is nothing impermissible [with the distinction], but in a diagrammatic presentation the distinction is too stark, and you fear that it will mislead others; that if some [feelings] are said to be perfectly good, while others are said to include both good and evil, you fear that others might question whether there are two kinds of feelings with two kinds of goodness.

• On the Third [Fourth][11] Section: That according to my letter, the Four Beginnings and Seven Feelings each have their own point of origin, and it's not just a matter of a difference in the way of speaking of them.

• On the Fifth Section: The fourth item in your quotes from Master Chu, that in the case of Mencius, he has singled out [the nature and described it in its original condition] while [Ch'eng] I-ch'uan included [the physical endowment] and essentially says that they are inseparable.

• On the Sixth Section:
The fifth item of your argument, that my letter's characterizing the Seven Feelings as externally stimulated by the physical
A36b form and not being the original substance of principle is extremely impermissible; that if such were the case, the Seven Feelings would be some thing apart from the nature, and so on; that Mencius being joyful and unable to sleep . . . how are these not the original substance of principle?
The seventh item of your argument, [my interpretation of] "as soon as you have them and are not able to exercise discernment."
The discussion at the end regarding the wrongness of my explanation concerning the point of origin and [each having its] particular focus.

• On the Twelfth Section: That Master Chu misunderstood the saying regarding the mind-and-heart as a matter of the already-aroused condition, and realized it only after a long time, and your discussion to the effect that [the passage concerning Master Chu's] talking about principle giving issuance or material force giving issuance was a chance statement and refers to only one side of the matter.

The above nine items are cases in which our views are different, and in the end I cannot accept your opinion.

Having thus summed up agreement and difference on the various issues, T'oegye says that there is no need for further discussion on the points where there is agreement or where he was mistaken and has already revised his position accordingly. The eight points where he and Kobong start the same but end up with different conclusions and the nine points on which there seems no agreement, however, are worth further discussion to see if they might not reach an accord. He begins his discussion with a few general comments and then takes up each point.

A37b   Indeed, that the Four Beginnings are not without material force or the Seven Feelings without principle is not only your assertion; I likewise say it. And it's not only you and I who say it— former Confucians have already said it as well. And it's not that they were forcing things in speaking so, but in the original flow and pattern of what is endowed by Heaven and received by humans, that is definitely the way it is.

Nonetheless, it is just this point that is involved in the area where our views start out the same but differ in the end. In your opinion, the Four Beginnings and Seven Feelings both combine
A38a   principle and material force. They are the same reality with different names and cannot be categorically differentiated in terms of principle and material force. In my view, one approaches their difference and sees in its midst that there is sameness; therefore, there are many cases in which the two may be spoken of in an undifferentiated manner. And one approaches their sameness and understands in its midst that there are differences; so with regard to that with respect to which one speaks, of itself it basically involves the dissimilarities of principle as the predominant factor or of material force as the predominant factor (*chu i chu ki*), so why is this not a rationale for categorically differentiating them?

Although admittedly there were faults in what I said previously, there was actually something behind what I was trying to get at. But your argument criticized it all, so that hardly a phrase or a word escaped intact. So now, even though I may again take up the discussion to explain and clarify what makes this so, I fear that it will not help me gain credibility, but only amount to an excess of apprehensiveness.

Items in Which the Beginning Is the Same but the Conclusions Are Different[12]

[1.] Your argument states: [In discussing] the nature of Heaven and Earth, one exclusively refers to principle; [in discussing] the physical nature, principle is mixed together with material force. . . . "These are the issuance of principle" is certainly the case; "these are the issuance of material force" does not exclusively refer to material force [cf. A8b].

I would say that as for the nature of Heaven and Earth, definitely, exclusively referring to principle, do you mean that at that moment there is only principle and there is no material force? The world has never had principle without material force, so it's not a matter of there just being principle. If that were the case, and one could still speak with exclusive reference to principle, then in the case of the physical nature, although it is a mixture of principle and material force, why should it be impermissible to speak with exclusive reference to material force? In the one case, principle is the predominant factor, and so one speaks of it from the point of view of principle; in the other, material force is the predominant factor, and therefore one speaks of it from the point of view of material force. This is what it means when, even though the Four Beginnings are not without material force, one only speaks of the issuance of principle, or when one only speaks of the issuance of material force, even though the Seven Feelings are not without principle.

[Kobong replies, B7a–8b]

When you hold that [the saying regarding] the issuance of principle cannot be changed but [the saying regarding] the issuance of material force does not exclusively refer to material force, how do you come up with this double assessment of a single way of speaking? If it actually is not a matter of exclusively referring to material force but rather combines a reference to principle, then

A38b

[Chu Hsi] should not have spoken of it paired in contrast with the issuance of principle.
[Kobong responds, B8a–8b]

[2.] Your argument says that, in the case of Heaven and Earth and men and other creatures, the distinction of principle and material force does not pose any problem, but in the case of discussing the nature, it is principle as descended into the midst of material force. If one discusses the feelings, it is the situation of the nature as descended into the psychophysical endowment, so they combine principle and material force and have both good and evil. Distinguishing them in terms [of principle and material force] is unsatisfactory [cf. A13b–14a].

A39a

I would say that considering the case of Heaven and Earth and man and other creatures likewise is not a matter of principle being outside material force. If one can make the distinction in that case, then in the case of the nature or of the feelings, although one says that principle is in material force or the nature is in the psychophysical endowment, why is it impermissible to distinguish them? For in man's single body, principle and material force combine, and so he is born. Therefore, the two have a mutually issuing function, and, moreover, they are interdependent in the issuing. Since it is a mutual issuance, one can see that each may have its particular role; they are interdependent, so one can see that both are included [in the issuing]. Since both are included, there is certainly an undifferentiated way of speaking of them; since each has its particular role, therefore there is nothing impermissible in a way of speaking that distinguishes them.
[Kobong responds, B7a–8b; B21a & ff]

"Mutual issuance" (hobal), introduced here, became a central issue in the debate over the years; it was attacked with particular vigor by Yulgok. The English translation here usefully picks up the ambiguity of the Chinese text; it is not clear whether it means they each have an issuing function, albeit they are interdependent in carrying it out, or whether "mutual" is just another way of saying "interdependent," that is, that they jointly have a role in the issuing function. In the light of the overall

development of his thought, it seems likely that T'oegye had the
former in mind, while Kobong, when he accepted this language,
was thinking in terms of the latter.

In discussing the nature, it is a situation of principle being in the midst of material force. If [in that situation] Tzu Ssu and Mencius could point out the original nature, and the Ch'engs and Chang Tsai could single out for discussion the physical nature, then in discussing the feelings, a situation in which the nature is in the midst of the psychophysical endowment, why in that case alone should it be impermissible to consider in each case whence it issues and so distinguish the Four Beginnings and Seven Feelings in terms of their point of origin? The matter of combining principle and material force and having both good and evil does not pertain

A39b only to the feelings: the nature also is like that. How can you take this as evidence that it is not permissible to distinguish them?

[Kobong replies, B8a]

[3.] Your argument states: The Seven Feelings also issue from humanity, righteousness, propriety, and wisdom [cf. A15b].

I would say that this is what I have called approaching what is different and seeing the similarity; in such a case, the two can, of course, be talked about in an undifferentiated manner. But we cannot say that there is only similarity without any difference.

[4.] Your argument states: It is not the case that there is a particular distinctive kind of feelings that only issues from principle and not from material force [cf. A16a].

I would say: The issuance of the Four Beginnings is, of course, not without the involvement of material force. However what Mencius was referring to in fact was not the aspect of their issuance by material force.

[Kobong agrees, B9a]

If we say that a reference to material force is included, then already it is no longer a description of the Four Beginnings. And, furthermore, how could you go on in your argument to say that the statement that the Four Beginnings are the issuance of principle should not be changed?

[5.] Your argument states: It's not that there is no such principle within, and a fortuitous stimulus from external things arouses [the mind-and-heart] to activity. And the Four Beginnings are also [like the Seven Feelings with respect to how they are aroused] [cf. A16a-16b].

A40a I would say: This thesis is, of course, correct. But in this paragraph your quotations from the *Record of Music* and the sayings of Master Chu all make use of what may be described as an undifferentiated manner of discourse. If, from this perspective, we attack a mode of discourse that makes analytical distinctions, there is no need to worry about a lack of ammunition. Nevertheless, the mode of discourse that makes analytical distinctions is not something I have personally invented out of thin air. In the world from the very beginning, there has been such a principle; the ancients originally had explanations of this sort. Now if we insist on holding onto one mode at the expense of the other, would it not be one-sided?

From the perspective of the undifferentiated manner of discourse, the Seven Feelings combine both principle and material force. This is clear enough without wasting too many words. But if we contrast the Seven Feelings with the Four Beginnings and discuss each in terms of its distinctive characteristics, the Seven Feelings are related to material force in the way the Four Beginnings are related to principle.

[Kobong challenges this, B9b–10a]

Their issuances each has their own systematic ramifications, and their names each have their particular point of reference. Therefore, we can follow their predominant factor and categorize them separately, that is all. I have never said that the Seven Feelings have nothing to do with principle, or that they are aroused according to a fortuitous encounter with external things. And the Four Beginnings are certainly no different from the Seven Feelings as regards being stimulated by things and then moving. It's only that in the case of the Four, principle issues them and material force follows it, while in the case of the Seven material force issues them and principle mounts it.

[Kobong questions the interpretation and suggests other wording, B10a]

This last sentence first expresses T'oegye's famous final formulation of the difference between the Four Beginnings and Seven Feelings. His formulation for the Seven Feelings is quite conventional: Chu Hsi himself introduced the language of principle mounting on material force in his discussion of the Diagram of the Supreme Ultimate, *and it became a common way of expressing the relationship of the concrete, active material force and transphenomenal, non-active principle. T'oegye's description of the Four Beginnings, however, seems to indicate some kind of originating active role for principle, a departure from convention that became the the main bone of contention.*

A40b   [6.] Your argument states: when it is aroused it mounts material force to be active. . . . The Four Beginnings are likewise a matter of material force [cf. 16b].

I would say: The Four Beginnings are also a matter of material force. You have time and again stressed this point, and now you have further cited Master Chu's responses to his students' queries; this matter is abundantly clear. However, do you think Mencius's point in explaining the Four Beginnings was likewise their issuance by material force? If it is viewed as material force, then in the expressions "the beginning of humanity," "the beginning of righteousness," "the beginning of propriety," "the beginning of wisdom," how are we to understand the four words humanity, righteousness, propriety, and wisdom? If there is even the slightest admixture of material force, what we have is no longer the original condition of pure Heavenly Principle. If they are seen as pure Heavenly Principle, then the beginnings that issue from them are definitely not like things compounded of a mixture of water and mud.

In your opinion, humanity, rightness, propriety, and wisdom are terms that apply to the not-yet-aroused condition, and, therefore, they are pure principle. The Four Beginnings are terms that apply to the condition after [the feelings] have been aroused; without material force they could not be active, therefore, they are also a matter of material force. In my humble opinion, even though we say that the Four Beginnings mount material force, the point Mencius was making was not their mounting material force, but only

A41a   their issuance by pure principle. Therefore, he spoke of the beginning of humanity and the beginning of rightness, and later wise men likewise spoke of him as "singling it out and speaking of only the good side."[13] If we insist that the Tao must include material force, the moment we speak of it [in that way], we are already wading in muddy water and all these passages that have been cited will be irrelevant.

Earlier thinkers have used the analogy of a man coming and going mounted on horseback for the way principle mounts material force in order to be active;[14] this was indeed appropriate. Without the horse, the man cannot come and go; without the man, the horse will miss the way. Man and horse are interdependent and inseparable. People refer to this situation from various perspectives. Some refer to it in a general way and speak of the going, in which case both the man and horse are implicated. This is like speaking of the Four and Seven in an undifferentiated manner. Others refer to the man going; in this case, it is not necessary to refer likewise to the horse, but the horse's going is implied. This is like the Four Beginnings. Others might refer to the horse's going; in that case, it is not necessary to refer likewise to the man, but the man's going is implied. This is like the Seven Feelings.

Now, having seen that I talk about the Four and the Seven separately, you time and again attack my position from the perspective of those who talk about them in an undifferentiated manner. This is like hearing someone talking about a man going or a horse going, and emphatically asserting that the man and horse are a unity, so one cannot speak of them separately. When you see me talk about the Seven Feelings from the perspective of the issuance of material force, you emphatically assert that they are also the
A41b   issuance of principle. This is like hearing someone speak of a horse going and insisting that he must mention the man going. When you see me speak of the Four Beginnings from the perspective of the issuance of principle, then again you emphatically assert their issuance by material force. This is like hearing someone speak of a man going and insisting that he must mention the horse going. This is precisely like what Master Chu described as playing a game of hide-and-seek. What do you think about this?

> *It is notable that the Chinese precedents for the imagery of the man mounted on a horse occur in the context of discussing the metaphysical or cosmological relationship of principle and material force. Its introduction here into a discussion of the derivative metaphysically and cosmologically grounded psychological theory is another matter: it leads to questions that do not arise in the cosmic context, such as pursuing the image in terms of the successful or unsuccessful control of the rider, the responsive qualities of the horse, and so on. The Neo-Confucian vision inserts humans entirely into the natural, cosmic framework, so philosophically what applies in the case of the cosmos should consistently apply also in the case of human beings. This is put directly to the test in this debate, which in an unprecedented way tries to work out the metaphysics of the functioning of the human psyche. The success or failure of various versions of the horse and rider image in achieving cosmic consistency brings out the systematic tensions and necessities inherent in a thoroughly cosmological view of human beings.*

[7.] Your argument states that if one pursues them back to their root and origin, then two different things are not originally intended [cf. 18b–19a].

I would say that if one discusses them from the point of view of their similarity, then it seems that two different things are not intended. But if you contrast them and pursue the matter back to its root and origin, then there really is a differentiation between principle and material force. How can one say that there is no difference?

[Kobong questions this, B9b–10a]

[8.] Your argument states: Whenever the word "nature" is used, it does not one-sidedly refer to material force. If I [i.e., T'oegye] say "one-sidedly referring exclusively to material force," you fear that it is not correct. And your argument says that [since I say] Tzu Ssu's discussing equilibrium and harmony was an undifferentiated mode of discourse, then how can the Seven Feelings not be a combination of principle and material force [cf. A19b]?

A42a   I would say that when the word "nature" is used [here], it is not used with no reference to material force, and rather in my explanation, the two words "one-sidedly" and "exclusively" do in the end seem problematic. Therefore, I have followed your advice and changed them.

[Kobong comments, B11a]

However, this is fundamentally different from the point at issue in the case of the Seven Feelings' combining principle and material force and being an undifferentiated mode of expression. Now you take this as a case of my explanation not having escaped inconsistencies, but in fact it is not an inconsistency. Since the point in question is not the same, what is said must also differ, that is all.

Items of Complete Disagreement

[9.] Your argument says: they are the same reality but with a different name; it's not that outside the Seven Feelings there are also the Four Beginnings. . . . The Four and the Seven do not mean different things [cf. A9b–10a].

I would say that one approaches them in their similarity and understands that there is actually a distinction between the issuance of principle and the issuance of material force and so gives them different names, that is all. If there is fundamentally no difference, then why do they have different names?

[Kobong questions this and similar expressions, B9b–10a]

Therefore, although one cannot say that apart from the Seven Feelings, there are in addition the Four Beginnings, I fear that it is impermissible for one to go on to regard them as not meaning different things.

[10.] Your argument states that in a general discussion there is certainly nothing impermissible in saying that the Four issue from principle and the Seven issue from material force, but by making a diagram and locating the Four in the principle circle and the Seven in the material force circle, the separation is too sharp and grievously misleads people [cf. 10b].

A42b

I would say that if it is permissible, it is totally permissible; if it is impermissible, it is totally impermissible. How could it be that there is nothing impermissible in distinguishing them as two issuances in a general discussion, but when one makes a diagram and distinguishes them with two locations, it suddenly becomes impermissible? What's more, in the diagram the Four Beginnings and Seven Feelings are in fact in the same circle, [the distinction being] abbreviated [to a difference of being arranged] in more inner or more outer positions, with separate annotations appearing side-by-side [below the circle], that is all. They were never located separately each in a different circle.[15]

[Kobong disagrees, B11a–11b]

[11.] Your argument states that when one is described as nothing but good and the other is described as including both good and evil, you fear that people might wonder whether there are two kinds of feelings or two kinds of good [cf. A11a].

I would say that the expressions "pure principle and therefore nothing but good" and "combines material force, therefore include both good and evil" are basically not contrary to reason. Those with understanding approach what is similar and understand the differences, and are also able to base themselves on what is different and understand the similarities. Why should we be so worried lest the ignorant misunderstand that we abolish words that are in accord with reason? But it happens that we are now using the expressions of Master Chu in the diagram, so these words have already been removed.

[Kobong disagrees, B11a–11b]

[12.] Your argument states that if one interprets the phrase in terms of [my] letter then the Four and Seven each has its own point of origin, and it's not just that the way of speaking of them is different [cf. A12a].

I would say that although they are alike in being feelings, they are not without a difference in point of origin; therefore, the ways they have been spoken of in the past are different. If there is fundamentally no difference in their point of origin, then what basis do those who speak of them have for differentiating them? As for Confucius's disciples not elaborating the matter fully or Tzu Ssu's speaking of them in their entirety, in these cases they certainly did not use a mode of explanation that had to do with point of origin. But when it comes to Mencius's singling out and explaining the Four Beginnings, how can one not describe it as

A43a

speaking of them with reference only to the one aspect of principle issuing? And if the point of origin of the Four is principle, as for the point of origin of the Seven, if it is not material force, then what is it?

A43b   [13.] Your argument instructs by quoting Master Chu's explanation that Mencius has singled out just the nature in his way of speaking, while I-ch'uan [Ch'eng I] included the physical endowment and says essentially they are inseparable [cf. A13a].

I would say that this passage, insofar as it says the nature is inseparable, thereby clarifies that the feelings cannot be separated [from the psychophysical endowment], that's all. Nonetheless, in your prior quotation from Master Chu, did it not say "Although it may at a given time be present in the midst of material force, nevertheless the material force is material force and the nature is the nature; they do not become mixed" [cf. A13a]? I would venture the opinion that Master Chu's approaching the matter of Mencius speaking in a way that singled out [the nature] and I-ch'uan's speaking in a way that combined [the nature and the psychophysical endowment] and so saying essentially they are inseparable is just what I have already described as seeing that there are similarities in the midst of differences. His approaching the case of the nature being in the midst of material force and saying that material force is material force and the nature is the nature, and they are not admixed with one another, is just what I have described as understanding differences in the midst of sameness.

The authoritative passages referred to here had the respective functions of, on the one hand, avoiding an overly dualistic view of li *and* ki *and, on the other, of using the duality of* li *and* ki *to preserve the Mencian doctrine of the good nature (*li*), while introducing a factor internal to the human constitution that could explain evil (*ki*). T'oegye's position can be understood as the outstanding historical test of whether the "not admixed" proposition merely preserved Mencius verbally or whether it could actually support the phenomenological and existential meaning carried by Mencius's original observations.*

[14.] Your argument states: My letter's describing the Seven

Feelings as being externally stimulated by physical form and so not the original substance of principle is particularly unacceptable. In that case, the Seven Feelings would be something external to **A44a** the nature. . . . Mencius's feeling of pleasure to the extent that he could not fall asleep . . . was this not the original substance of principle [cf. 17a]?

I would say: At first I erroneously said, "how could it be that what is externally aroused is physical form, but its issuance is the original substance of principle?" What I meant was, how could it be reasonable that when they are aroused it is a matter of material force, but when it comes to their issuance it is a matter of principle? But since I felt that the expression was not absolutely clear, I have already changed it.

Now in your letter the text [of my remarks] is changed to state directly, "[the Seven Feelings] are externally stimulated by physical form and so are not the original substance of principle,"[16] but this is a far cry from my original intention. This is followed directly by your indictment: "In that case, the Seven Feelings would be something external to the nature." Then do you mean that when Master Chu said, "As for the Seven Feelings, these are the issuance of material force,"[17] he likewise meant the Seven Feelings are something outside the nature? Generally speaking, there are cases where principle issues and material force follows, so one can speak of these in a way that takes principle as the predominant factor, that is all; that does not mean that principle is external to material force. The Four Beginnings are such a case. There are cases in which material force issues and principle mounts it, so one may speak of them in a way that takes material force as the predominant factor; but that does not mean that material force is external to principle. The Seven Feelings are this kind of case.

That in the Four Beginnings, "principle issues and material force follows," while in the Seven Feelings, "material force issues and principle mounts it," became the final wording of T'oegye's position, and as such the phrases became a constant reference point for later generations.

The pleasure of Mencius, the anger of Shun, the sorrow and joy of Confucius—these are the issuances of material force in compliance with principle. There is not even an iota of obstruction; therefore the original substance of principle is in a condition of undifferentiated wholeness.

A44b

[Kobong questions this, B9b–10a]

The cases of ordinary people being pleased when they see their parents, or being sad when they are in mourning, are also the issuance of material force in compliance with principle. However because of irregularities in the material force [of ordinary people] the original substance of principle cannot be in its pure and integral condition.

If we discuss the question from this angle, even though we regard the Seven Feelings as the issuance of material force, what problem will there be as regards the original substance of principle? Furthermore, how will there be anything to worry about regarding there being no connection between physical form on the one hand and the feelings and nature on the other?

[15.] Your argument says: "Your [i.e., T'oegye's] letter states: 'As soon as we have them but are not able to exercise discernment, the mind-and-heart will not attain its proper condition. And only after they have issued with proper measure can they be called harmonious.' Then this makes the Seven Feelings quite superfluous and useless. And on the contrary [Chu Hsi's original reference was not to the Seven Feelings but to] things that may harm the mind-and-heart" [cf. A17b].

I would say that with regard to this matter, the words and intent of my previous explanation were in the wrong context and therefore were problematic. Now I have amended this.[18] I am indebted to you.

A45a

But your letter also objects to the "As soon as we have them but are not able to exercise discernment" passage on the grounds that it is a matter that pertains to the rectification of the mind-and-heart and quoting it as evidence regarding the Seven Feelings is a quite different matter. This seems to be the case, but in fact it is not so. For although this passage belongs to the chapter on the rectification of the mind-and-heart, this one sentence to the effect that joy and anger, worry and fear may not be permitted [a fixed] place in the mind-and-heart, is an explanation of the problem of the mind-and-heart, that is all. It has not yet addressed the question of rectifying the mind-and-heart.

Indeed, the reason these four easily become harmful to the mind-and-heart is really that [the feelings] issued preconditioned by material force, although they are originally good, easily slip towards evil, and thus it is so, that is all. As for the Four Beginnings, which are the issuance of principle, how has there ever been this kind of problem?

[Kobong completely disagrees, B12a–13a]

> *This is one of the clearest indications of what T'oegye is trying to get at with his distinction. His idea seems to be that many of our responses (the Seven Feelings) are intrinsically rooted in the particularity of our physical being and may easily become self-centered. But some responses (the Four Beginnings) are rooted profoundly in the human nature that is common to us all. Though both kinds of feelings emerge only through our concrete physical being, their different origin puts them on an essentially different footing.*

Moreover, how can you say that the mind-and-heart might have something about which it commiserates, but not attain its proper condition, or the mind-and-heart might have something about which it feels shame and dislike, but not attain its proper condition? The *Letter on Calming Human Nature* says: "As for that in the human mind-and-heart which is easily aroused but difficult to control, anger is the most extreme. But at a time when one might be angered, one can just forget the anger and reasonably consider the right and wrong of the case; so one can also see that external temptations need not be hated."[19] So, what is referred to as "easily aroused and difficult to control," would that be principle, or would it be material force? If it were principle, why would it be difficult to control? It is material force, and therefore it gallops fast and is difficult to restrain, that is all. Moreover, if anger were the issuance of principle, then how would you have what was said about forgetting anger and considering principle instead? But

A45b

because it is the issuance of material force, he spoke of forgetting anger and considering principle instead. This is what is meant by reining in material force with principle. If this is so, then in what way is my quoting this passage as evidence that the Seven Feelings belong to the material force category not pertinent?

[16.] [Your argument] is the same as the discussion toward the end of the previous section: the mistake of my theory that based on its point of origin the referrant of each has a predominant factor and emphasis. And you further say that this argument is not just a matter of impermissible terminology, but rather you suspect that with respect to the reality of the nature and the feelings and the practical application to preserving [one's inborn good dispositions] and exercising reflection [in activity], in all these respects it has impermissible [implications] [cf. A18a].

I would say: The thesis regarding the point of origin and predominant factor can be clarified through the whole context of our debate and needs no further discussion here. As for the [questionable points] regarding terminology or the reality of the nature and the feelings, where there was the least bit of uneasiness on my part I have already carefully corrected it, partly because of your instruction and partly because of my own realization. Seeing that the problematic points have been eliminated, its meaning is luminously transparent and clearly manifest, like open windows in all directions or the ringing of jade. It comes close to managing to avoid the problem of [indiscriminately] lumping things together. As for the application to preserving [one's inborn good dispositions] and exercising reflection [in activity], although I cannot venture to be presumptuous about it, I suspect that there is nothing that goes so far as to be seriously unacceptable.

A46a

[Kobong comments, B11a]

[17.] Your argument says Master Chu misunderstood the saying regarding "mind" as referring to the after-aroused condition and after a long time finally realized [the truth], and you theorize that the single saying regarding the issuance of principle and the issuance of material force is a chance expression and one-sided reference [cf. 22a–22b].

I say that when I consider what you are getting at in this

section, it seems as if you regard this explanation [i.e., the saying regarding the issuance of principle and the issuance of material force] of Master Chu's as insufficient. This is extremely unsuitable. Indeed, the recorded sayings of the Ch'engs and Master Chu certainly have not escaped occasional discrepencies and errors: in the elaboration of the meaning of certain expressions and explanations, there are certain junctures where the understanding of the one who recorded it could not penetrate and in some cases even missed the original meaning. But in this particular section, we have a case of a few sentences of concise words directly conveying the content of a secret transmission, with Han-ch'ing [Fu Kuang] as the recorder, and he was in fact one of the foremost of Chu Hsi's disciples. In such circumstances, to make a mistake in recording would be utterly unlike a man such as Fu Han-ch'ing!

A46b   If, my friend, in the course of your ordinary reading of the *Yü-lei* you had seen this passage you certainly would not have found anything to doubt in it. But now since you regard my thesis as wrong and are strongly arguing against it, and this passage of Master Chu's is what I take as my basis, you cannot help criticizing it; then you can judge my words wrong and be believed by others. Thus it reaches the pass that you even implicate [Master Chu in my error]. This is undoubtedly my fault for presumptuously dragging in a quotation from earlier [authorities]. Nevertheless, with regard to these kinds of matters, my friend, although I concede your courage in taking responsibility for upholding the true Tao, isn't there a problem of lacking disinterestedness and humility? If one goes on like this, will it not perhaps lead to the abuse of forcing the words of the sages and worthies to agree with your own opinion? Yen Hui "had, but seemed not to have, was full, but seemed empty,"[20] knowing only the inexhaustibility of truth [moral principle] and not considering whether it was his [opinion] or another's as making any difference; I'm not sure whether or not such an attitude can still be found.

[Kobong denies this criticism and strongly criticizes T'oegye's harshness here, B14a–14b]

Master Chu was the most firm and courageous man in a hundred generations, but if he realized there was a slight error in his view or something uncertain in what he had said, he was always glad to hear about it and immediately amended it. Even in his late years, when his path was exalted and his virtue fully realized, he behaved so. How can one who has hardly set forth on the path of sage learning already be so inclined to regard himself as match- **A47a** lessly occupying the highest position?! For one should know that true firmness and true courage are not a matter of being osten- tatiously forceful in explanations, but rather in amending faults and not being begrudging in hearing what is right and immediately accepting it.

Reply to Kobong's Postscript

[A47a–48b, mainly dealing with omitted portion of Kobong's postscript (cf. note, A26b), has been omitted]

A48b   . . . And as for the thesis that the Four Beginnings also in- volve cases that are not in perfect measure, although it is very novel, nevertheless this is not what Mencius was originally getting at. Mencius's intention was just to indicate [the feelings] that are the pure emanations of humanity, rightness, propriety, and wis- dom [i.e., the constituent characteristics of human nature], so that by explaining them he might make manifest that the nature is fun- damentally good and therefore the feelings are likewise good, that is all.

But now you feel the need to put aside this correct and proper original intention, and pull it down to the level of the common, ordinary man, concocting an explanation that the issuance of his feelings is not perfectly measured. Indeed, a man's feeling shame and dislike for what he should not feel shame and dislike, or feel- ing something is right or wrong when it should not be felt right or wrong—all this is the effect of the turbidity of material force. How could one refer to this kind of vulgar thesis as grounds for confusing the status of the Four Beginnings as the pure issuance of **A49a** Heavenly Principle! This kind of theory not only is of no benefit in clarifying the true Tao, but on the contrary I fear that it would be harmful to pass it on as instruction for later students.

[49a–51a omitted][21]

A51b   But what you are critical of is not a matter of my expressions being problematic, but rather is entirely concerned with the fact that my words arise from a mistaken point of view. I would characterize this as a matter of having reached full understanding and realization in looking into principle and having achieved full perfection in the expression of it. As for me, after having put ten years of effort into it, I have barely attained anything like that. I am not able to really understand it, and therefore my expressions have been so problematic. In your case, it seems as if you can make a decision with the stroke of your brush in the time it takes for a brief chat. The difference between the one who understands and the one who does not seems more than just thirty miles here![22]

But how can we further argue this out with more talk? We ought just to follow steadily the course of night and day and work on it for another ten years or more, and then, considering what each of us has managed to see, perhaps a proper assessment can be determined. If even then it still cannot be determined, then the matter will have to wait for a latter-day Chu Hsi to appear and then the rights and wrongs can be decided.

Or, as I have heard, if one's paths (*tao*) are the same, then with a single word, there is a meeting of minds, but if [the paths] are not the same, a lot of talk on the contrary further obstructs the [true] path. The learning we two pursue cannot be said not to be the same. But we have not been able to have a meeting of minds with a single word, and we have already talked so much, I fear that it may not serve to clarify things but rather to shake up and damage them. Nonetheless, there are also two scenarios here. In the one case, if the spirit is one of seeking to win and not of seeking to understand the truth, then to the end there can be no rationale for an agreement, and it will just come to looking for the world's public opinion, that is all. But in the case of those who set their minds on understanding the truth (*tao*), with neither side [just seeking to maintain] its own opinions, then there must eventually come a day when they come to agreement. This is possible only for superior men of accomplished understanding who love the pursuit of learning.

I am old and so dim-witted; I greatly fear that my pursuit of learning may have receded, and my private ideas taken over, so that I have recklessly spoken words of no profit, so that I have placed myself beyond the generous bounds of your encouragement and admonition. I just hope that you will forgive my presumption and show your kindness; that, in the end, would be a great good fortune for me!

CHAPTER 6

Kobong's Response to the Second Letter

T'oegye's remarks toward the end of his letter (A51b) were meant to be a gentle termination of further discussion concerning the Four Beginnings and Seven Feelings question. But Kobong responded in the first month of 1561 with an even longer, forty-three-page letter. In his introductory comments (B1a–3b, omitted here), he praises T'oegye's letter, exults in the high degree of agreement they have already reached, and expresses the desire to press on to conclude the few items that remain to be settled. He then comments on the revised draft of T'oegye's first letter and goes on with an itemized review of the various sections of T'oegye's second letter. As regards the revised draft, he expresses satisfaction at T'oegye's more explicit recognition of the mutual presence and interdependence of principle and material force in both the Four Beginnings and Seven Feelings, but he is still uneasy about the discussion contrasting them in terms of principle and material force, for its tone seems to communicate a one-sided emphasis. But his more serious objections still focus on Section Six of the letter; we will begin with his remarks on this section.

[Introductory remarks, B1a–3b, omitted]

On the Revised Draft of the First Letter [cf. A29a–33a]

[Introductory remarks affirming changes omitted]

B4a   . . . But as for your expressions "When external things arrive, that which is most susceptible to stimulus and the first to move"

and "what is externally aroused [i.e., the Seven Feelings] is physical form," and so on [cf. A30b], I fear that they cannot but be
B4b   regarded as somewhat one-sided. I venture to request the happiness of another letter explaining it more exactly.

And as for [your saying that I say] "the Four Beginnings and
Seven Feelings do not mean something different" [A31a], or
again, "on the contrary you say that the Four Beginnings and
Seven Feelings have no different referent" [A32a], and so forth,
that does not seem like my original meaning, for my initial explanation just said that the Four Beginnings and Seven Feelings from
the start never meant two things. And now when you put it as
"they do not mean something different," or "they have no different
referent," the meaning of the phrases turns around what I originally meant.[1]

And again when you say, "You do not seek the point of origin of the Four Beginnings and Seven Feelings, but generalize in
terms of their combining principle and material force and including
both good and evil" [A31b–32a]—that was not my original intention. For in my explanation, I said that the Four Beginnings are
those of the Seven Feelings that issue and are perfectly measured;
they are the same reality, but with a different name [cf. A9b]. This
certainly is not a matter of "generalizing in terms of their combining principle and material force and including both good and evil."
But now it seems not to have received close scrutiny.

And your instruction further says, "In your opinion the Four
Beginnings and Seven Feelings both combine principle and material force. They are the same reality with different names and cannot be categorically differentiated," and so on [A37b–38a]. Here I
B5a   have completely failed in communicating my meaning to you.
How can that be! How can that be! Rather, in my former letter, I
said that the Seven Feelings combine principle and material force
and include both good and evil. Therefore, those of them that issue
and are perfectly measured are rooted in principle and are never
not good. Those of them that issue and are not perfectly measured
are admixed with material force and sometimes devolve into evil.
And the Four Beginnings themselves are a matter of principle and
are good. Therefore, I regard them as the same reality with a dif-

ferent name as those of the Seven Feelings that issue and are perfectly measured, and so on [cf. A9b]. What I said before and after that time and again—all is in line with this.

And among those items there was also included my thesis that the Four Beginnings likewise are a matter of material force. And in your argument you said, "It does not make sense to say that [the Four Beginnings] are within us as pure principle, but at the moment they issue they are mixed with material force" [A30b], and that was in order to clarify the fact that the Four Beginnings are not without material force. Also, there was my explanation that there are cases in which the Four Beginnings are not perfectly measured. For the feelings of ordinary people are bound up with the desires that go with the psychophysical endowment, so sometimes as soon as Heavenly Principle issues and shows itself, it is distorted and obscured by the psychophysical endowment and its desires, so it likewise has cases of not being perfectly measured. It's not that I definitely mean to be saying that the Four Beginnings likewise combine principle and material force and involve both good and evil.

As for saying that they cannot be categorically differentiated, what I mean is this. From wise men of earlier times on, there has been the settled thesis that the Seven Feelings combine principle and material force and include both good and evil. And now if one speaks of them in contrast with the Four Beginnings in terms of the Four Beginnings being a matter of principle and the Seven Feelings a matter of material force, then the side of the Seven Feelings that is principle, on the contrary, is taken up by the Four Beginnings, and saying that they include both good and evil seems as if it just comes from material force. When it comes to the meaning conveyed in making a diagram and setting up symbolic representations, this seems still quite imperfect, that is all. It's not that I mean that it is absolutely impermissible. That is not the case: it's just that in general explanations saying the one is the issuance of principle, the other is the issuance of material force, is like speaking of the nature of Heaven and Earth and the physical nature, so what is impermissible about that? I beg clarifying explication of this.

B5b

[B5b–6b omitted][2]

B6b   On the First and Second Sections [of T'oegye's Response]

Now I would suggest that the instruction presented in these two sections is all subtle, profound, and exact; it directly and completely penetrates to the heart of the matter and leaves one with my
B7a   meager and narrow vision no room to continue his chattering.[3] For as you say, it's not that there is only principle, and so if in that case one may exclusively refer to principle, then when it comes to the physical nature, although it is a mixture of principle and material force, why should it be impermissible to speak of it with reference to material force [cf. 38b]? And, as you say further, in approaching a consideration of Heaven and Earth, men and other creatures, it also is not a case of principle being outside material force [cf. 39a]. If, in that case, one can differentiate in speaking of them, then in the case of the nature or the feelings, although one says principle is in the midst of material force or the nature is in the midst of the psychophysical endowment, why should it be impermissible to differentiate between them? As a delineation of the boundaries of principle and material force that clarifies explanations that distinguish between them, these words can be said to be one hundred percent precise and exhaustive.

Nevertheless, in my humble opinion, if one pursues the matter in this vein, then it also seems not quite free of a slight overemphasis on the side of drawing distinctions. Therefore, at times it one-sidedly stretches the real intent of the words and sayings of the ancients. I beg to try to explain this more exactly. Master Chu says:

> As for the nature of Heaven and Earth, it is the original ponderous [substance] of the Supreme Ultimate, the single fundament of the myriad differentiated [manifestations]. As for the physical nature, it is born of the interacting revolutions of the two forces [i.e., yin and yang]. There is a single fundament and a myriad differentiations.[4]

That is, the physical nature is principle as descended into the midst of the psychophysical endowment, that is all; it's not that there is

B7b another separate nature. I would say that the nature of Heaven and Earth is a holistic explanation from the point of view of Heaven and Earth [i.e., the universe]; the physical nature is an explanation from the point of view of what [specifically] men and other creatures are endowed with. The nature of Heaven and Earth might be likened to the moon in the sky, and the physical nature would be like the moon reflected in water. Although the moon as in the sky and in the water is not the same, nevertheless insofar as it is the moon, it is one and that is all. But now if one were to say that the moon in the sky is the moon, and the moon in the water is water, would that not constitute an unavoidably problematic assertion?

When it comes to distinguishing principle and material force from the point of view of Heaven and Earth, then the Supreme Ultimate is principle, and yin and yang are material force. When one distinguishes principle and material force with reference to man and other creatures, then the firm [i.e., yang] and the compliant [yin, female] and the five constants[5] are principle, and the two vital souls[6] and the five organs are material force. As for principle and material force in [concrete] things, although one may say that they are indistinguishably mixed and inseparable, this nevertheless does not prevent the two of them from each being its individual self. Therefore, I said that in distinguishing principle and material force with reference to Heaven and Earth and men and other creatures, there certainly is no problem as regards the individual thing [i.e., principle or material force] remaining as an individual thing.

But if one discusses the matter with regard to the nature, then truly it is like the moon in the sky and the moon in the water. For, **B8a** in that case, the one moon is spoken of differently according to its location, that is all; it's not that there is another separate moon. Now, if one categorizes the moon in the sky as moon and the moon in the water as water, does not this way of speaking of it involve one-sidedness? And this is all the more so in the case of what are called the Four Beginnings and the Seven Feelings, for that is a matter posterior to principle having descended into the psychophysical endowment; [continuing our comparison], it would be like the radiance of the moon in the water. As for the radiance, in the case of the Seven Feelings there is brighter and dimmer, while the Four Beginnings are exclusively the bright. But the

Seven Feelings have [the difference of] brighter and dimmer because of the water's clarity or turbidity; and when the Four Beginnings are not perfectly measured, then although the radiance is bright, it is not free from the movement caused by waves. I humbly beg that you reflect on these ideas and consider what they may mean.

Moreover, in the first section you say that [if I was correct, then Master Chu] should not have paired it in contrast with "the issuance of principle" [cf. 38b]. In my opinion, when Master Chu says, "The Four Beginnings, these are the issuance of principle; the Seven Feelings, these are the issuance of material force,"[7] it is not a contrastive exposition (*taesŏl*) but a consecutive exposition (*insŏl*). For a contrastive exposition is like speaking of left and right, in which the two stand in opposition to one another; a consecutive exposition is like speaking of higher and lower, in which there is a dependent connection between the two. The words and sayings of the sages and worthies definitely involve a difference between contrastive and consecutive expositions and one must take that into consideration.

B8b

In the next section, you ask, why just in this case should it be impermissible to approach each from the point of view of its issuance and distinguish the respective points of origin of the Four Beginnings and Seven Feelings? In my opinion, the Four Beginnings and Seven Feelings alike both issue from the nature, so I fear that one cannot approach each from the point of view of its issuance and distinguish them. I would humbly ask that you make a diagram that contrasts the nature of Heaven and Earth and the physical nature, and then again make another that contrasts the Four Beginnings and the Seven Feelings.[8] Then if after carefully comparing and considering them and determining how it all is, it would be a great happiness if you would instruct me and clarify the matter for me.

On the Third Section

See the discussion of the preceding and following sections; no need for repetitious discussion.

On the Fourth and Sixth Sections

B9a   Comment: Originally, because the expressions in your letter had a one-sided emphasis, I superficially responded in order to clarify the fact that material force is not absent in the Four Beginnings. I did not intend to say that what Mencius was referring to included material force [cf. 39b]. My explanation definitely did state that at the moment of the nature's issuance [as feelings], if material force does not take over, the original goodness [of the nature] can be directly fulfilled. This truly is what Mencius refers to as the Four Beginnings. For although what are called the Four Beginnings cannot be said not to have material force, at the moment of their manifestation, the original substance of Heavenly Principle genuinely presents and reveals itself without a trace of deficiency; it seems like something devoid of material force. It might be compared with the moon reflected in a pure lake: since the water is especially clear and transparent, the moonlight seems even more brilliant, and the surface and the interior are totally translucent, as if there were no water. Therefore, we can say that they are issued forth by principle. We may take a perspective that includes material force, but is that the point Mencius meant to convey?

As for the playing of hide-and-seek that you criticize, although that certainly was not my original intention, my mode of expression does involve this problem. It is something that I myself have constantly regretted, but I have not been able to avoid. I sincerely hope that you, master, will [continue to] call my attention to it so that I may be warned.

B9b   On the Fifth, Seventh, Ninth, Twelfth, and Fourteenth Sections

I would respectfully suggest that these five sections are truly the most essential parts of your argument and the most complex and refractory part of our discussion. Therefore, I would venture to combine them and discuss them all together.

The fifth section says their issuances each have their systematic ramifications, and their names each have their particular points of reference [cf. A40a]. The seventh section says, "If one pursues the matter back to its root and origin, then there really is a differentiation between principle and material force" [cf. A41b]. The ninth section says that there is actually a difference between the issuance of principle and the issuance of material force, and thus they are differently named [cf. A42a]. The twelfth section says, "If the point of origin of the Four is principle, as for the point of origin of the Seven, if it is not material force then what is it?" [cf. A43a]. The fourteenth section says: "The pleasure of Mencius, the anger of Shun, the sorrow and joy of Confucius, these are the issuances of material force in compliance with principle" [cf. A44a–44b].

In general, all these passages advocate explanations that differentiate. I would not venture a rash, forced explanation; rather it would be fitting just to follow the expressions used in your argument and clarify them, that is all.

I venture to ask, when joy and anger, pleasure and sorrow issue forth and are perfectly measured, do they issue from principle or do they issue from material force? And as for those that

B10a issue forth and are perfectly measured, those that are the "there is no respect in which they are not good"[9] kind of good, is that the same as the goodness of the Four Beginnings, or is it different? If you regard [feelings] that issue forth and are perfectly measured as issuing from principle and their goodness as in no way dissimilar [from that of the Four Beginnings], then as for all that you have said in these five sections, I fear that it cannot yet be regarded as exact. If you regard [feelings] that issue forth and are perfectly measured as issuing from material force and their goodness as involving some dissimilarity [with that of the Four Beginnings], then as for the explanations of the *Chung-yung chang-chü*, the *huo-wen*, and the other explanations that all clarify the Seven Feelings as a combination of principle and material force, how can all these fall into place? And the repeated assertions in your own argument that the Seven Feelings combine principle and material force would also be empty words.

As for the right and wrong of these two sides, which should

be followed and which rejected, there must necessarily be a way to resolve it. I am not sure what you will finally think about it. But if in this matter there is no adjudication, then as they say, we will have to wait for a latter-day Chu Hsi [to solve it]; it is not something I would venture to claim to know. I beg you to give it your most careful consideration.

And as for the two sentences "In the case of the Four, then principle issues and material force follows it" and "in the case of the Seven, then material force issues and principle mounts it" [cf. 40a], they are exceedingly refined and precise. But in my mind, the meaning of these two is that in the case of the Seven Feelings, they combine [principle and material force], and in the case of the Four Beginnings, there is only principle issuing them—just the one side. Rather than these two sentences, I would like to emend it to say, "As for the issuance of the feelings, in some cases principle moves and material force is together with it; in other cases material force is stimulated and principle mounts it"—express it like that. But again, I am not sure what you would think of it.

B10b

When Tzu Ssu spoke [of the Feelings] in their entirety, he certainly was not using an explanation in terms of their point of origin; as for when Mencius singled out and explained the Four Beginnings, although one might describe it as referring to principle issuing them, just one aspect, as for the Seven Feelings, Tzu Ssu had certainly already spoken of them as combining principle and material force. How can one, on the basis of what Mencius said, suddenly change [Tzu Ssu's position] to material force, just one aspect? I fear that these propositions cannot yet be simply regarded as settled.

When material force is compliant with principle and issues without a single bit of obstruction, then it is the issuance of principle. If you wish to find some issuance of principle outside this, I fear that the further you go with such conjecture and groping, the more fruitless it will be. This is all the ill effect of overemphasizing modes of explanation that differentiate between principle and material force. In my former letter, I mentioned it and now I am repeating it; if you say it is not so, then Master Chu's statement "When yin and yang and the five agents mix together but do not

B11a

miss their proper lead, then it is principle"[10] also cannot be accepted. I beg that you carefully examine this matter.

> *This last paragraph pinpoints a critical point of interpretation regarding the issuance of principle. Kobong's interpretation is perfectly in line with the conventional Ch'eng-Chu school formulation of the interdependence of principle and material force, and it is the position that will be eloquently elaborated and defended by Yulgok. But it is also clear that the critical feature in such an issuance is really the compliant/noncompliant, pure/turbid condition of material force (see Kobong's further remarks on this below, B16b). It seems that in this interpretation the dynamic development or spontaneous movement to manifest the characteristics that make us human implicit in Mencius's Four Beginnings is lost. T'oegye's formulation of the issuance of principle seems to be an attempt to mean something more than the conventional interpretation; it is a move that leaves more room for Mencius at the price of logical consistency in his metaphysics.*

On the Eighth and Sixteenth Sections

Comment: What I reported as the theory you expressed in your letter was not without inaccuracies. And the statement that there were unacceptable implications regarding the application to preserving [the mind's good dispositions] and exercising reflection [in activity] was a casual and reckless expression. I certainly should be concerned about it. However, at the time I resorted to such an expression, I did have something to which I was calling attention. Now, perusing the items [of your letter], I see among them that my theses regarding the Seven Feelings' not being exclusively a matter of material force and regarding good and evil's being not yet determined have undeservingly met with your approval, and you have also already amended the first letter. Thus my wild and groundless remarks of the previous day have become pointless. There is no need to pursue it further. I humbly present this for your lofty scrutiny.

On the Tenth and Eleventh Sections [cf. A42b]

B11b

When I said that there was nothing impermissible [with those expressions] in a general discussion, I was speaking of them as a consecutive exposition. When I said that when one makes a diagram it is impermissible, I was speaking of them [as appearing to be] a contrastive exposition. If one insists on speaking of them as a contrastive exposition, then even though they might be Master Chu's original explanation, I fear [that these expressions] cannot avoid being misunderstood. What do you think?

On the Thirteenth Section: Mencius's Singling Out and I-ch'uan's Speaking Inclusively [cf. A43b]

The five passages I quoted from Master Chu were meant to explain the original nature and the physical nature. The idea was that multiple discussions would mutually clarify one another; I never meant to quote these to explain that the Feelings cannot be differentiated. You, on the other hand, being intent on asserting separateness, reject this passage, calling it into question and putting it among the items about which, in the end, you cannot accept my opinion. Even in the case of someone as ignorant as I, how can you put this among the unacceptable items when it is the words of Master Chu? I fear that this is not the attitude of selflessly seeking to clarify the truth.

If one must take this passage and investigate it, then Mencius's singling out and speaking of the nature in its original condition seems like approaching the moon in the water and referring

112a

from it to the moon in the heavens. I-ch'uan's speaking inclusively of the psychophysical endowment is like approaching the moon in the water and just referring to its being the moon. This is what is meant by saying they are inseparable. As for material force remaining material force and the nature still being the nature, this is really just like the water's just being the water and the moon the moon. They certainly do not become admixed with one another. This is my view of the matter. I humbly beg that you indicate the mistake, and let me know if it is alright or not.

**On the Fifteenth Section: If as Soon as we Have Them but
are not Able to Exercise Control** [cf. A44b]

I have respectfully examined the teaching in this section, and
although it is repeated in various ways, it seems to be a forced explanation and difficult to comprehend. For the original meaning of
the passages in the *Commentary [on the Great Learning]* and the
Huo Wen was nothing like this, and now as for what you said, I do
not understand how you can have that view of it. Since I have
already had the favor of your teaching, I cannot venture to do
anything but exhaustively present my own ignorant ideas.

I would suggest that in the text of the commentary section of
the *Great Learning*, in the passage that says, "If one has (*yu*) anger, then [the mind-and-heart] does not attain its proper condition," and so on and so forth, all the four times the character "*yu*"
[have/is] occurs, it is used not in the sense of "happens to be," but
B12b   rather in the sense of "deliberately have." Therefore, the *Commentary* said, "If you have but one[11] and are not able to exercise discrimination," and so on, and the annotation paraphrases "have" as
"wait," "remain," "inclined to stay." And again the *Yü-lei* says:

> It's just that these several [feelings], pleasure, fear, anger, and
> worry just should arise anew [each time]; they may not be per-
> mitted to have a prior place in the mind-and-heart. And consid-
> ering the matter, it's not just these few items that are like this:
> whenever we try by prior manipulation to make sure that some-
> thing will be a certain way it doesn't work. If a man determines
> in his mind that he must be solemn and stern and enduring, after
> a little while he just has tunnel vision fixed on this intention
> being present and not being lost; then he is all bound up by it.
> Or another man determines in his mind to be warm, generous,
> and kind; after a little while he just has tunnel vision fixed on
> this intention being present and not lost, and then he slips into
> continual temporizing measures and a life of destitution.[12]

Considering these passages, it seems to me that they are not in line
with your interpretation. Moreover, explaining the problem of the
mind-and-heart makes a person exercise discernment in order to

rectify it and so it pertains to the rectification of the mind-and-heart. On what basis can you say that it is not yet involved with the explanation of the rectification of the mind-and-heart?

And the intention of this chapter [of the *Great Learning*] is to enable a person's mind-and-heart to attain its proper condition, like an empty, clear mirror or like the level balance of a scale, so when it is aroused by things its response will be entirely in perfect measure. If, when commiseration is not in order, one beforehand has commiseration, or, when one should not be feeling shame and dislike, one beforehand has this disposition, then I think these also are cases where the mind-and-heart has not attained its proper condition.

B13a

As for what the *Letter on Calming Human Nature* said about forgetting one's anger, it was referring to cases in which it is not in proper measure. I do not understand the way you quoted it in your discussion. But if this seems not the case, then as for the *Yü-lei* passage that says:

> When there is a matter that is joyous, one may not just forget all about what he should be joyous about due to the onset of feelings of anger. When there is something to be angry about one may not just forget all about the anger because some joyful matter comes up.[13]

I do not know how in the end this fits with [what you interpret] the *Letter on Calming Human Nature* to say.

So I am eagerly awaiting your illumination of these complexities. I am in suspense and avidly desire your response.

On the Last Section [cf. 46a]

I have humbly and carefully read over the last paragraph of your letter, which explains my problem, completely [exposing] its grave and inveterate nature. If it were not for your accomplished virtue by which you can be concerned about others as you would be for your own self, how could you have reached this! What great good fortune for me! For my whole life, this should be engraved in my heart and not neglected or forgotten.

B13b

Nevertheless there are also my own sincere thoughts on the matter, which I cannot venture not to express for your hearing, if perchance you would deign to consider them. In my previous letter, my quoting the letter of Master Chu to the various gentlemen of Hunan and so on [cf. A22a–22b] was really meant to clarify how one who studies cannot one-sidedly hold on to a single saying, and that is all. It certainly was not intended to imply some insufficiency in what Master Chu explained, nor did it speak critically of the recorder; I do not understand how you could have admonished me in this vein. My thoughts are so unsettled and disturbed I cannot find a reply.

But in what I said, the words "words spoken by chance" and "refer only to one side" [cf. A22a] seem involved in what you censure. But these words were used to contrast with the terms "furnished with full context" and "complete and well-rounded," not because I ventured to impute insufficiency [to Chu Hsi] or speak critically [of the recorder]. I once read a passage in the *Chung-yung huo-wen* that said:

> The sayings of the sages and worthies certainly have no cases of a beginning that does not have any conclusion. One who studies must do his utmost to make himself disinterested and to focus all his thoughts in order to discern what conclusion [is being moved toward]; it is not enough to hold onto a single saying and immediately regard the matter as settled.[14]

How is this saying anything but impartial and clear! If someone is not able to make himself disinterested and to focus all his thoughts, but immediately grasps a single saying to make it the interpretive principle for all the other explanations, then his abuse in forcing the words of the sages and worthies to fit his own ideas would certainly be indescribable.

B14a

On the contrary, [your expression] "a direct conveyance of a secret transmission" seems questionable. Throughout his life, Master Chu wrote works and established his words to teach those who came after as lucidly as the sun and moon that move in the heavens to make anyone with eyes able to see. What reason could there be for him to hold back his real meaning secretly in order to transmit it to a single man! I suspect that the mentality of sages and worthies is not as mean-spirited and narrow as that! If in the end it were that way, there would truly be nothing to blame in the saying "You can show people your embroidered ducks, but do not take up your golden needle with the idea of giving it to others."

And your letter says: "If, my friend, in the course of your ordinary reading of the *Yu-lei* you had seen this passage, you certainly would not have found anything to doubt in it. But now, since you regard my thesis as wrong and are strongly arguing against it and this passage of Master Chu's is what I take as my basis, you cannot but also criticize it; then you can judge my words wrong and be believed by others. Thus it reaches the pass that you even implicate [Master Chu in my error]. This is undoubtedly my fault for presumptuously dragging in a former explanation" [A46a–46b].

B14b   My reckless foolishness and ignorance certainly are rightly [censured] as guilty of an offense against my senior. Nevertheless, if I am to be guilty of an offense on grounds such as this [i.e., the above quotation] then I cannot venture to rest content. Is not what you say a matter of being overly severe in reproaching others and treating others without empathy? Also, it seems close to infringing against [the custom of] compensating with extreme impartiality when one feels disposed to be critical of someone.

In general, when it comes to people's pursuing learning, although there are differences of the shallow and the profound, nevertheless the disposition is definitely one of wanting everyone to arrive at the good; it is not one of desiring to place oneself in the position of being a crafty deceiver externally seeking a reputation for learning. If one were to pursue learning with this kind of predisposition, then finally what sort of disposition would it be that was being called "pursuing learning"! This kind of charge even a man of no substance who shifts with the times would not be willing to take, and it is right that I not venture to rest content with it. I humbly beg you to think over and reconsider this matter. I have no way to settle my extreme shame and upset.

On the Reply to My Postscript: On the Thesis That the Four Beginnings Are Not Perfectly Measured [cf. A48a]

[The first section, 14b–16b, dealing with untranslated portion of the postscript, is omitted, cf. note, A26b]

I would suggest that when one sees the statement that the Four Beginnings are not perfectly measured, it seems strange, and **B16b** I suspected that you might not accept it. And now it has indeed turned out that way. Nonetheless, my explanation never said that Mencius's original intention was anything like that. It's just that the feelings of the ordinary man cannot help but be that way, that is all. And this thesis also has a precedent. A passage in the *Yü-lei* discussing Mencius's Four Beginnings says:

> As for commiseration and shame and dislike, there are cases when they are perfectly measured and cases when they are not perfectly measured. If one feels commiseration when it is inappropriate, or when it is inappropriate to feel shame and dislike one feels shame and dislike, then these feelings are not perfectly measured.[15]

This case of taking up what Mencius already said and clarifying what he did not fully elaborate is extremely significant; one cannot but profoundly consider it. For Mencius, in clarifying the principle that human nature is good and explicating it in terms of the Four Beginnings, stated in a general way the "nothing but good" aspect, but he did not explain fully the precise details. From ancient times, the sages and wise men have been few, and the foolish and unwise many, those born with understanding few, and those who must study to learn or learn only with painful effort many. But if one is not a sage born with understanding, how can the issuance of the Four Beginnings in one necessarily manage to conform to the purity of Heavenly Principle? I suspect it will not manage to be free from the distorting influence of the psycho-physical endowment and selfish desires.[16]

B17a   Now if one does not consider this, and just regards the Four Beginnings as nothing but good and wishes to broaden and fulfill them, then I fear his understanding of the good will be incomplete and his vigorous practice somewhat off the mark. How much more so in the case of someone like me, who is at the very lowest level of the ordinary, with a psychophysical endowment that is coarse and impure and who is endlessly bound up by selfish desires! If during the course of daily life I constantly exercise exacting discernment about the beginnings [of feelings] that issue, then there are a few that are perfectly measured, and many that are not. Therefore, I ventured to inform you of this in my previous letter in hopes that it might perhaps meet with agreement. Now when I examine your instruction on the matter, I see that what you say is perfectly fitting. Nevertheless, when I consider the matter in the light of the *Yü-lei* passage, I fear it cannot just be cut off at this point. I beg you to carefully reexamine it.

[Sections 17a–21a, dealing with omitted portions of T'oegye's response are omitted, cf. note, A49a]

B21a   When I consider the explanations you have sent for my instruction, they involve a problem of one-sidedness and partiality. This is directly related to the mistake of overemphasizing the distinction of principle and material force, as in the second section [of your letter], which says:

> In man's single body, principle and material force combine, and so he is born. Therefore, the two mutually have an issuing function and moreover in issuing they are interdependent. Since it is a mutual issuance, one can see that each may have its particular role; they are interdependent, so one can see that both are included [in the issuing]. [A39a]

B21b   This in fact is the very source of the objection and calls for profound consideration.

Indeed, the relationship of principle and material force is certainly difficult to understand, and it is likewise difficult to talk about. The wise men of earlier times always regarded it as a problem—how much more so for us later scholars! Now I would like to give a rough description of my views in hopes of refinement and clarification from you, but my words do not fit my intent, and so it

is difficult to give a direct explanation. Thus I will try a simile. [Principle in material force] may be compared to the sun in space. Its light is constantly renewed through all ages. Although clouds and fog may arise, its light is not thereby darkened. It is steadfastly just as it is, but it is obscured by the clouds or fog, and so it is impossible for there to be uniformity in clear or overcast weather. When the clouds disperse, and the fog rolls back, then again it radiates all over the earth below, but its light is not thereby increased, and it is still just as it is. Principle being in material force also is like this. This principle of pleasure, anger, sorrow, and joy, commiseration, shame and dislike, yielding and deference, and right and wrong are combined together in the midst as the true actuality of the original substance. At times, they may be distorted and obscured by the physical nature and its desires; then as for the original substance of principle, although it steadfastly remains as it is, in its manifestation there are then the distinctions
B22a of the darkened and the clear, the true and the false. If one completely rids oneself of the hindrance of the physical nature and its desires, then as for the original substance's movement into activity, is it not like the sun's shining all around on the earth below? Master Chu says:

> As for material force, it is able to condense and have creative activity; principle, on the other hand, has no feeling or intent, no deliberation or creative activity. It's just that in the condensing and collecting process of material force, principle is then in its midst.[17]

[This is] his direct description of this matter. Now, if you say that they mutually have an issuing function and in the issuing, moreover, they are interdependent, then principle, on the contrary, does have feeling and intent, does have calculation, does have creative activity.

Furthermore, it seems that the two, principle and material force, are like two men dividing and possessing the interior of the single mind-and-heart, alternating in control and both being [in turn] leader and follower. This has to do with the foundation of the whole system, so even a hair's-breadth discrepancy is impermissible: if one is off on this, everything else will also be off. I beg you to give me detailed evidence on this matter.

CHAPTER 7

Kobong's Postscript Explanation of the Four Beginnings and Seven Feelings

> *T'oegye responded to Kobong's letter in 1562 with a short letter politely declining further discussion. After a time, Kobong wrote back. He accepted T'oegye's decision, but noted that he had followed T'oegye's advice to reflect quietly on the question during times of leisure, and in this way he had achieved some insights that took him beyond his previous understanding. He wrote up his final understanding of the whole matter in a "postscript explanation" and a "general summary," and sent these along to T'oegye for his examination. T'oegye's correspondence with Kobong on various matters continued, but he first mentions these two pieces in an undated letter following one written in 1566. Thus it seems likely that Kobong's Postscript and General Summary were composed about 1566, that is, after four years of further reflection on the issues.*

B23b   As for the explanation of the Four Beginnings and Seven Feelings, formerly I considered cases in which the Seven Feelings issued and were perfectly measured as not different from the Four Beginnings. Therefore I doubted their distinct categorization in terms of principle and material force. I regarded the issuance of the feelings as combining principle and material force and having both good and evil; but the Four Beginnings speak [of the feelings] with exclusive reference to those that are the issuance of principle and are nothing but good, while the Seven Feelings speaks [of the feelings] definitely as referring to their combining principle and material force and having both good and evil. If one categorizes the Four Beginnings as principle and the Seven Feelings as material force, that means that the aspect of the Seven Feelings that is principle is, on the contrary, taken over by the Four Beginnings, and those spoken of as having both good and evil seem to come only from material force. In terms of the language and expressions involved, this is something that must be considered dubious.

Nonetheless, after repeated investigation with reference to Master Chu's statement that "the Four Beginnings, these are the issuance of principle; the Seven Feelings, these are the issuance of material force,"[1] in the end I realized that there was something that did not fit [with my view]. Thus I thought it through again and understood that in my former way of explaining the matter there were points that were inexact and that my investigation was not yet complete.

B24a Mencius's discussion of the Four Beginnings posited that people all have the Four Beginnings in themselves, so we might know to expand upon and fulfill them all. Indeed, with respect to having these Four Beginnings and wanting to expand upon and fulfill them, it is certainly so that "the Four Beginnings, these are the issuance of principle." Master Ch'eng's discussion of the Seven Feelings took the feelings from the point of view that when they flame up, the more they run wild and the nature is destroyed. Therefore, realizing this, one restrains his feelings and makes them conform to the norm; in this respect, is it not likewise so that "the Seven Feelings, these are the issuance of material force"? When one looks at it in this way, the categorization of the Four Beginnings and Seven Feelings in terms of principle and material force is not itself a matter one need doubt, and one must understand that the terms "Four Beginnings" and "Seven Feelings" each have their rationale.

Nevertheless, those of the Seven Feelings that issue and are perfectly measured are from the start no different from the Four Beginnings. For even though the Seven Feelings may be categorized as material force, principle is certainly of itself in its midst. When they issue and are perfectly measured, they are the nature that is the Heavenly Mandate, the fundamental substance; in such a case, how could one characterize them as the issuance of material force and differentiate them from the Four Beginnings? *(As for what you said in your letter about the joy of Mencius, the* **B24b** *anger of Shun, and Confucius's sorrow and pleasure being cases in which material force issues in compliance with principle without the least bit of obstruction, and each [kind of feelings] having their own point of origin, and so on, are all matters I feel are still questionable. The [Doctrine of the Mean] characterizes [the Seven Feelings] when they "issue and are all in perfect measure" as the "universal Tao."* [2] *But in the end could one characterize the universal Tao as the issuance of material force, as suggested by what you say?)* [3] This also must be understood.

Master Chu once said: "When one discusses the nature of Heaven and Earth, one speaks with exclusive reference to principle; when one discusses the physical nature, then one speaks in terms of principle mixed together with material force." [4] Really this is the principle issuing/material force issuing thesis. I already used this quotation [cf. A8b] in connection with maintaining that saying [of the Four Beginnings] "these are the issuance of principle" is a matter of speaking with exclusive reference to principle, while saying [of the Seven Feelings] "these are the issuance of material force" is a matter of speaking in terms of principle and material force admixed. [This view] does not seem very unreasonable, but it did not meet with your considered approval; was this not perhaps because my way of expressing it was not clear? What you say in your argument about the distinction between the Four Beginnings and Seven Feelings being like the difference between the original nature and the physical nature in the case of the nature does not seem any different than the view [I was presenting]. I do not understand why you do not look into it, but rather regard it as among the items in which our basis is the same but the conclusions different [cf. A38a].

For indeed what is called the physical nature is a matter of speaking in terms of principle and material force as admixed. That is, since it is a matter of the original nature as descended into the **B25a** midst of material force, it is therefore characterized as an admixture [of the two]. Thus the physical nature when it is good is the same as the original nature; it's not that there is a separate nature.

So when I say that cases when the Seven Feelings issue and are perfectly measured are the same reality as the Four Beginnings but with a different name [cf A9b], I suspect that there is nothing that violates reason.

[Closing paragraph omitted]

CHAPTER 8

Kobong's General Summary of the Four Beginnings and Seven Feelings

Master Chu says:

B25b
> Man receives the equilibrium of Heaven and Earth to be born; his not yet aroused condition is pure and fine, perfectly good with all principles present therein: this is what is called the nature. But having such a nature, he has such a form, and having such a form, he has such a mind-and-heart, and it cannot but be stimulated by other things. When it is stimulated by things and moves, then the desires of the nature emerge, and with this good and evil diverge. The desires of the nature are what is called feelings.[1]

These words are actually an interpretation of the meaning of movement and quiescence in the *Record of Music* [in the *Book of Rites*]. Although they are simple, these words completely present the rationale involved in explaining the nature and the feelings; one could say that they are exhaustive and could not be improved upon.

But then what it calls feelings are joy, anger, sorrow, fear, love, hatred, and desire [i.e., the Seven Feelings],[2] and these are the same feelings as what the *Doctrine of the Mean* terms joy, anger, sorrow, and pleasure. Indeed, since "having this mind-and-heart one cannot but be stimulated by other things," we can see that the feelings are a combination of principle and material force. Since "it is stimulated by things and moves . . . and with this good and evil diverge," we can also see that both good and evil are involved. When joy, anger, sorrow, and pleasure issue, and all are in perfect measure, that is what is called principle, the good; and when their issuance is not in perfect measure, that is beccause the psychophysical endowment is one-sided and involves what is not good.

B26a   As for what Mencius called the Four Beginnings, it is a matter of approaching the feelings that combine principle and material force and involve both good and evil, and singling out and speaking of those that issue from principle and are perfectly good. For Mencius was clarifying the truth that the nature is good, so one can understand that he was speaking of the Four Beginnings as issuing from principle and being perfectly good.

Master Chu has also said, "The Four Beginnings, these are the issuance of principle; the Seven Feelings, these are the issuance of material force."[3] Indeed, the Four Beginnings issue from principle and are perfectly good; calling this the issuance of principle certainly can be regarded as indubitable. The Seven Feelings combine principle and material force and involve both good and evil, so their issuance, although it is not exclusively a matter of material force, likewise is not without an admixture of the material force aspect; therefore, calling this the issuance of material force is really like the explanation concerning the physical nature. For although the nature is originally good, its having descended into the endowment of material force means it is partial and unbalanced; therefore, it is referred to as the physical nature. Although the Seven Feelings combine principle and material force, principle is weak while material force strong, so [it happens that principle] does not control it and [the issuance] easily devolves into evil; therefore, [the Seven Feelings] are referred to as the issuance of material force.

B26b   Nonetheless, those that issue and are perfectly measured are the issuance of principle and are perfectly good, so from the start they are no different than the Four Beginnings. But the Four Beginnings are only a matter of the issuance of principle. Mencius's intention was actually a matter of wanting to get people to enlarge upon and fulfill them, so one who pursues learning, with respect to the issuance of the Four Beginnings, must endeavor to have a personal realization of it in order to enlarge upon and fulfill them. The Seven Feelings are an issuance that combines principle and material force, and that which is the issuance of principle at times is not able to master material force and the current proceeding from material force likewise, on the contrary, obscures principle. So one who pursues learning, with respect to the issuance of the Seven Feelings, must exercise self-reflection in order to overcome and order them. This also is the way in which the terms Four Beginnings and Seven Feelings each have their rationale. If one who pursues learning can work it out from the basis of this understanding, then he will have more than half the matter thought out.

"And someone asked: It appears to me rather that joy, anger, love, dislike, and desire seem close to humanity and righteousness." And Master Chu replied: "They certainly have aspects in which they resemble one another."[4] His saying "they certainly have aspects in which they resemble one another," instead of directly saying that they resemble one another, means that his intention is to be found in the "they certainly have."[5] Those who discuss the matter nowadays for the most part put joy, anger, sorrow, and pleasure alongside humanity, righteousness, propriety, and wisdom, and do not understand what Master Chu really intended. For since the notions of the Seven Feelings and Four Beginnings each express a particular meaning, I fear that one may not mix them together as a single explanation. One must also understand this.

In a letter of 1566(?)[6] in the course of discussing various matters, T'oegye also mentions Kobong's Postscript and General Summary and indicates his satisfaction with them. He also says that he will have to rethink his position on joy, anger, and so forth, in the case of sages and wise men, and his position on differentiating the Four Beginnings and Seven Feelings in terms of their point of origin as well. This seems to indicate a shift toward accepting Kobong's proposition that the Four Beginnings are no different than the Seven Feelings when they issue in perfect measure. Kobong's General Summary in particular does a masterful job of explaining the rationale for distinguishing the Four Beginnings and Seven Feelings as grounded in essential but different aspects of the self-cultivation process, and this in large part meets T'oegye's concerns on the matter. Kobong thus can now verbally support the differentiation T'oegye was arguing for, but he never changed his position on the issues at the core of the controversy, which had to do with his objection to any real distinction in the mode of origination of these feelings. On the contrary, it is T'oegye, whose verbal distinction is being upheld, who seems to be making the more substantive concession at the end.

Such was not to be the case, however. Two years later, in 1568, T'oegye composed for the instruction of the king a short work, the Ten Diagrams on Sage Learning *(Sŏnghak sipdo), which came to be regarded as his final masterpiece. In the sixth chapter, he presented both verbally and pictorially an explanation of the issuance of the feelings that essentially reiterates his position in his second letter of the debate. The centerpiece is still the assertion that in the case of the Four Beginnings "principle issues and material force follows," while in the case of the Seven Feelings "material force issues and principle mounts it." That is, his attempt to express a difference in terms of principle and material force in the origination of these feelings remains unchanged. As we turn now to the second round of the debate, we shall see that it was sparked in turn by Ugye's response to reading this passage in the* Ten Diagrams.

CHAPTER 9

Ugye's First Letter to Yulgok on the Four-Seven Debate

> *The text used for this translation is taken from* Yulgok chŏnsŏ
> *(The Writings of Yulgok), where Yulgok's letter appears first,
> and the letter of Ugye to which it replies is appended. Here they
> are translated in chronological order, beginning with Ugye; the
> reader will note, however, that the running pagination to the
> original text reflects this reversal, that is, the letters of Ugye
> have page numbers higher than those of Yulgok's replies. I have
> taken the liberty of adding a numerical sequence to the titles of
> these letters and using in them the names "Ugye" and "Yulgok"
> rather than the nomenclature of the* Yulgok chŏnsŏ. *Interlinear
> annotations made by Ugye and Yulgok appear in italics enclosed
> in parentheses.*

9.36b   It has been raining and overcast here without cease. I have
been wondering about your situation, whether or not it is clear and
harmonious, and thinking continuously of you. In the appended
pages of your last letter, you asked for a reply indicating how
things are.

Recently, I have been reading over the discussion set forth by
T'oegye in the Diagram of the Mind-and-Heart, Nature, and Feelings in his *Ten Diagrams on Sage Learning*. The middle section
reads:

> As for the feelings that are the Four Beginnings, principle issues
> them and material force follows it. Of themselves they are
> purely good and without evil; it is only when the issuance of
> principle has not yet reached its termination and is disrupted by
9.37a   > material force that they can devolve into what is not good. In the

109

case if the feelings that are the Seven [Feelings], material force
issues them and principle mounts it. In this case, likewise there
is not evil, but if the issuance of material force is not perfectly
moderated and obliterates principle, then it is uncontrolled and
becomes evil.[1]

Looking into this theory, [one finds that] it regards the issuance of
principle and material force as at first entirely without evil, and
says that with the imperfect moderation of material force, there
comes the devolution into evil. The explanation of the human
mind and the Tao mind is already like that with respect to distinguishing the issuance of principle and of material force, and from
ancient times on, sages and worthies have all respected it. So
might it be that, in itself, there is nothing excessive in T'oegye's
theory? I wish that you would take on this problem and enter into
mortal combat with it, using your utmost intent and greatest exac-
titude in solving my dull misperceptions. Such is my ceaseless
prayer.

The mind-and-heart with its empty spiritual character and its
consciousness is one, and that is all. How is it, then, that there are
two terms for it, the "human mind" and the "Tao mind"? It is
because the one arises from the self-centeredness of the psychophysical component, while the other originates in the correct principle of the normative nature.

> *This is a slight paraphrase of Chu Hsi's words in his preface to
> the* Doctrine of the Mean. *His description of the human mind as
> "arising from the self-centeredness of the psychophysical com-
> ponent" and the Tao mind as "originating in the correct princi-
> ple of the normative nature" will play as central a role in the
> Ugye-Yulgok debate as the* Yü-lei *passage on the Four Begin-
> nings and Seven Feelings did in the Kobong-T'oegye debate.
> The passages suggested to both Ugye and T'oegye the same
> thing: a differentiation in terms of principle and material force
> in the origination of value-differentiated forms of activity in the
> human psyche.*

The issuance of material force is not the same, and so as functions "the perilous" and "the subtle"[2] are each different. Therefore, the terminology cannot but be twofold.

If that is so, is the case of what is termed the "Four Beginnings" and the "Seven Feelings" the same? As for the Tao mind, it would be permissible to refer to it as the Four Beginnings; but when it comes to the human mind, to call it the Seven Feelings would be impermissible. Moreover, the Four Beginnings and Seven Feelings are spoken of in terms of their being the issuance of the nature, but the human mind and Tao mind are spoken of in terms of being the issuance of the mind-and-heart. Between them, there is this difference regarding terminological category and meaning.

9.37b

I hope that you will grant me a word disclosing the real point here. In the point of origin whence the human mind and Tao mind issue, there is certainly the dissimilarity of the predominance of *ki* (*chu ki*) and the predominance of *li* (*chu i*). Even in the time of Yao and Shun, when there was not much theorizing, there was already this thesis. Since the main ideas of the sages and worthies all involved this bifurcation, when it comes now to making a diagram of the Four Beginnings and the Seven Feelings in terms of being issued by principle and being issued by material force, what is impermissible in that? The mutual issuance of principle and material force has been an established principle in the world, and so is not the insight of Master T'oegye in itself proper? Nevertheless, his explanation in terms of material force following [principle] or principle mounting [material force] truly pushed it too far and seems to be mistaken as regards the rationale of the terminology.

In my humble opinion, if one contrasts the Four and Seven with each other, it is permissible to describe the Four as being issued by principle and the Seven as being issued by material force. But in making his diagram of the nature and the feelings,[3] he should not have made such a differentiation; rather he should have just put both the Four and the Seven within the "feelings" circle and said: "The Four Beginnings are spoken of with reference to the side of the Seven Feelings that manifests principle; that in the Seven Feelings which is not perfectly moderated is a matter of material force being excessive or deficient so [the feelings] de-

9.38a   volve into evil." Then he would not have gotten sunk in [theories] about the issuance of principle and of material force, and likewise he would not have had the problem of differentiating them like two [separate] branches, would he? I beg you to investigate this matter carefully and enlighten me on it.

CHAPTER 10

Yulgok's Response to Ugye's First Letter

9.34b   The theories of the sages and worthies are of various types, and each type has its particular point. If one tries to take one type as the standard for the other or combines dissimilar types, then one of them will lose its proper meaning.

The mind is single; using [diverse] terms for it such as "the Tao mind" and "the human mind" is because of the distinction between our normative nature and our psychophysical constitution. The feelings are single; speaking of them in some cases as "the Four [Beginnings]" and in others as "the Seven Feelings" is because of the difference between speaking with exclusive reference to principle and speaking of it as combined with material force. Thus the human mind and the Tao mind cannot be combined, but rather are related in the same fashion as end and beginning. The Four Beginnings are not able to include the Seven Feelings, but the Seven Feelings include the Four Beginnings.

As for the subtlety of the Tao mind and the perilousness of the human mind, Master Chu's explanation completely explains it: "The Four Beginnings do not have the comprehensiveness of the Seven Feelings, while the Seven Feelings do not have the genuineness of the Four Beginnings."[1] In the light of this, what is the meaning of my humble view that they are related to each other as end and beginning?

Now, [the dispositions of] man's mind-and-heart emerge directly from the correctness of the normative nature, but sometimes
9.35a   they are not able to conform to it and follow it out, but rather become interfused with selfish intentions. When this happens, it is

113

a case of beginning with the Tao mind and ending with the human mind. Or sometimes they emerge from the psychophysical constitution but do not diverge from correct principle; in this case, there is certainly no departure from the Tao mind. Or sometimes they diverge from correct principle but recognize the mistake and become ordered and subdued and do not follow the selfish desires. When this happens, it is a case of beginning with the human mind and ending with the Tao mind. For the human mind and the Tao mind refer inclusively to both the feelings and the intention; they do not refer only to the feelings. The "Seven Feelings" are a comprehensive reference to the movement of man's mind-and-heart as composed of these seven. The "Four Beginnings" are a selective reference only to the good side of the Seven Feelings. This is definitely not like the kind of explanation in which "the human mind" and "the Tao mind" [are terms that] stand as contrasting alternatives.

Moreover, "feelings" are a matter of the emergent motion; [the term] does not include the matter of calculation. This is a further difference from the way the human mind and Tao mind may be related as the beginning and end [of a process]. How can one force the matter and make them comparable?

If one wants to explain things in terms of a two-sided [contrast], he should follow the human mind/Tao mind thesis; if he wants to explain only the good side, then he should follow the Four Beginnings thesis; if he wants to inclusively explain both good and evil, then he should follow the Seven Feelings thesis. There's no need to try to fit a square peg in a round hole and get everything confused.

The Four Beginnings and Seven Feelings are just like the original nature and the psychophysical nature. "Original nature" is **9.35b** a term that does not include a reference to the psychophysical endowment. "Psychophysical nature," however, does include the original nature. Thus [in a similar manner] the Four Beginnings cannot include the Seven Feelings, but the Seven Feelings include the Four Beginnings. Master Chu's reference to one as issued by principle and the other as issued by material force was just a summary statement. How could he have imagined that later scholars would make it the object of such extreme analysis! It is acceptable if those who study interpret it flexibly.

Moreover, Master T'oegye, having already taken goodness and run it back to the Four Beginnings, then goes on to say that the Seven Feelings likewise are without evil. In that case, there would likewise be good feelings apart from the Four Beginnings. In accord with what do these feelings issue forth? Mencius was presenting a general outline; therefore, he only mentioned commiseration, shame and dislike [for evil], deference and reverence, and the sense of right and wrong. As for the other good feelings' being [likewise] the "Four Beginnings," those who study should be able to pick up the implication and understand it. Where are there any human feelings that are good but are not based on humanity, righteousness, propriety, and wisdom? Feelings that are good already belong to the Four Beginnings, and if, apart from the Four Beginnings, there are other good feelings, then that would amount to man's mind-and-heart having two roots. Could that be true?!

In general, the condition before [the mind-and-heart] is aroused is the nature; after it is aroused, it is feelings. When it is aroused and engages in consideration and calculation, it is will. The mind-and-heart is the master of the nature, feelings, and will. **9.36a** Therefore the conditions of being not yet aroused, already aroused, and exercising calculation can all be referred to as the mind-and-heart. That which does the arousing-issuing is material force; that whereby there is the arousing-issuing is principle. The cases of its issuance directly emerging from correct principle with no interference from material force are "Tao mind," which is the good side of the Seven Feelings. In cases where at the moment of issuance material force has already interfered are the "human mind," which is the combination of good and evil in the Seven Feelings. In cases where one recognizes the interference of material force, exercises careful discernment, and follows correct principle, the human mind has taken direction from the Tao mind. When one is not able to exercise careful discernment and consider one's direction, then feelings overcome, the passions are inflamed, and the human mind is all the more perilous, and the Tao mind all the more subtle [and hard to realize]. The exercise of careful discernment, the yea or the nay, are entirely a matter of the will; therefore, in cultivating oneself nothing has priority over making the will sincere.

Now, if one says that in the case of the Four Beginnings principle issues and material force follows it, while in the case of the Seven Feelings material force issues and principle mounts it, then principle and material force are as two things, one of which is anterior, one posterior, and they stand in contrast as two branches each with its own distinct emergence. How does this not amount to there being two foundations of man's mind-and-heart?!

As for the feelings, although there are a myriad varieties, which of these is not the issuance of principle? It's just that some are disrupted by material force and interfered with, while others are not disrupted and submit to principle; therefore, there are the differences between good and evil. If one can come to a personal realization of the matter in these terms, he will be close to a perfect understanding.

9.36b As for the explanations you presented in the supplement, in general you had it right. But what you said about the Four Beginnings and Seven Feelings being the issuance of the nature, while the human mind and Tao mind are the issuance of the mind-and-heart seems to regard the problem of the mind-and-heart and the nature as two [distinct] branches. The nature is the principle within the mind-and-heart. The mind-and-heart is the vessel filled with and holding the nature. How could there be a distinction between the issuance of the nature and the issuance of the mind-and-heart?! The human mind and the Tao mind are both issued by the mind-and-heart by means of the nature; those that are disrupted by material force are the human mind and those that are not disrupted by material force are the Tao mind.

CHAPTER 11

Yuglok's Response to Ugye's Second (Missing) Letter

In the missing letter[1] Ugye raised questions about the presence of evil in the quiescent condition before the mind-and-heart is aroused. This leads Yulgok into a discussion of the relation of li *to good and evil on the concrete, phenomenal level, which is one of the critical issues in the background of this entire debate. Yulgok's presentation of his ideas on this topic, one of the most difficult in Neo-Confucian thought, is unusually bold and clear. His own note at the end recognizes that his statements could well be controversial, for this issue is rarely addressed with such forthrightness.*

9.38a   That in the substance of the mind—the condition before it is aroused—one can likewise speak of there being both good and evil is a great misunderstanding. [As the first chapter of the *Doctrine of the Mean* says]: "The condition before pleasure, anger, sorrow, and joy are aroused is called equilibrium. . . . Equilibrium is the Great Foundation [of the world]." How could [this condition] involve what may be spoken of as both good and evil? But in the case of the mind-and-heart of ordinary people, if it is not darkened and befuddled, then it is scattered and dissipated; the Great Foundation has not been established, and therefore one cannot describe [their condition] as equilibrium. But if by chance for the blink of an eye [their mind-and-heart] might be in a not-yet-aroused condition, then since it is the condition before being aroused, the integral substance [of the mind-and-heart] is, in its calm clarity, no different from that of a sage. But in a moment it loses its sub-

Diagram of the Mind-and-Heart, the Nature, and the Feelings

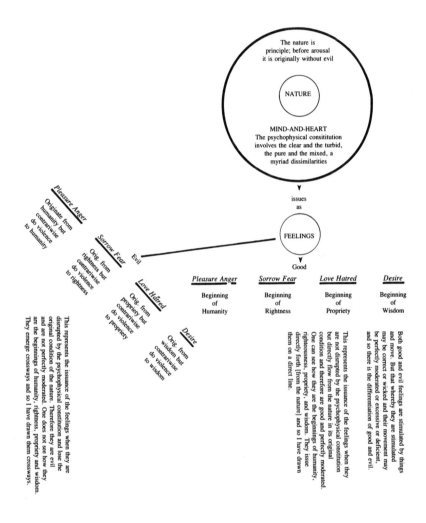

The nature is
principle; before arousal
it is originally without evil

NATURE

MIND-AND-HEART
The psychophysical consititution
involves the clear and the turbid,
the pure and the mixed, a
myriad dissimilarities

issues
as

FEELINGS

Good

Evil

Pleasure Anger

Sorrow Fear

Love Hatred

Desire

Beginning
of
Humanity

Beginning
of
Rightness

Beginning
of
Propriety

Beginning
of
Wisdom

Pleasure Anger
Originate from
humanity but
contrariwise
do violence
to humanity

Sorrow Fear
Orig. from
rightness but
contrariwise
do violence
to rightness

Love Hatred
Orig. from
propriety but
contrariwise
do violence
to propriety

Desire
Orig. from
wisdom but
contrariwise
do violence
to wisdom

This represents the issuance of the feelings when they are
disrupted by the psychophysical constitution and lose the
original condition of the nature. Therefore they are evil
and are not perfectly moderated. One does not see how they
are the beginnings of humanity, rightness, propriety and wisdom.
They emerge crossways and so I have drawn them crossways.

This represents the issuance of the feelings when they
are not disrupted by the psychophysical constitution
but directly flow from the nature in its original
condition and therefore are good and perfectly moderated.
One can see how they are the beginnings of humanity,
righteousness, propriety, and wisdom. They issue
directly forth [from the nature] and so I have drawn
them on a direct line.

Both good and evil feelings are stimulated by things
and move. But that whereby they are stimulated
may be correct or wicked and their movement may
be perfectly moderated or excessive or deficient,
and so there is the differentiation of good and evil.

stance, and darkness and dissipation ensue; therefore, it cannot attain its proper equilibrium. It is darkened and dissipated because of being disrupted by one's psychophysical constitution. It is permissible to say that [the mind-and-heart] may be disrupted by the psychophysical constitution and so cannot establish its Great Foundation. But it is a great mistake to say that at the time before it is aroused, there are likewise the incipient shoots of evil. For the

9.38b time when it may be darkened or it may be dissipated cannot be described as the not-yet-aroused condition [of the mind-and-heart].

9.39a Master Ch'eng said: "In the psychophysical endowment with which man is born, principle has good and evil."[2] This was much to the point in awakening people. Those words break it open. What he speaks of as principle refers to principle as it mounts on material force and becomes active; it does not refer to principle in its original condition. In its original condition, principle is certainly purely good, but when it mounts material force and becomes active, it is differentiated in countless ways. Since there is both good and evil in the psychophysical endowment, principle likewise has both good and evil.

Indeed, principle in its original condition is purely good, but when it has mounted material force it is disparate, not uniform. From the purest, cleanest, most noble of things to the filthiest and most base, there is nothing in which principle is not present. And when it is in the purest and cleanest, then principle likewise is pure and clean; when it is in the filthiest, then principle is likewise filthy. It is permissible to regard the filthy condition as not being the original condition of principle; but it is a mistake to conclude that filthy things do not have principle. For the original condition is that of principle's unity. The condition of having become active is that of its manifold differentiation. One definitely may not set aside its becoming active and seek principle in its original condition elsewhere; but it would likewise be wrong to regard principle as having both good and evil as its original condition.

It is most fitting to investigate personally the words, "Principle is one but diverse [in active manifestation]."[3] Understanding only the unity of principle and not recognizing its diversity

9.39b amounts to the Buddhist [mistake] of taking function for the nature and madly giving oneself over to dissoluteness. Understanding only the diversity and not recognizing the unity of principle is the same as Hsün Tzu and Yang Tzu regarding the nature as evil or as a mixture of good and evil.

As I think it over again, the proposition in your last letter[4] that at the time before [the mind-and-heart] is aroused there are also the incipient shoots of what is not good seems even more greatly in error. This truly is the root of your problem in not understanding the Great Foundation. The not-yet-aroused condition is the nature in its original state, the wondrousness of the Supreme Ultimate, equilibrium, the Great Foundation. If, in this condition, there are likewise the incipient shoots of what is not good, it would mean that the sage alone has the Great Foundation, and it is absent in the ordinary man. Mencius's explanation of the nature as good would be vacuous, lofty chit-chat, and people could not become like Yao and Shun. Why did Tzu Ssu, in that case, not say, "The condition before the Superior Man's pleasure, anger, sorrow, and joy are aroused is called equilibrium," instead of making a general statement that the condition before pleasure, anger, sorrow, and joy are aroused is called equilibrium? This is absolutely wrong, and it is urgent that you should quickly amend it.

[Postscript]: In the above discussion there are elements that former worthies have not yet discovered. If I had not met you, my discernment could not easily have gotten to this point. If we agree on this, then there is nothing on which we do not agree. As for **9.40a** those who are called scholars nowadays, how could there but be some who are bright and good at argumentation. But I have not seen many who could talk about this matter, and likewise there would be few who could see this discussion and not think it strange and laugh at it.

CHAPTER 12

Ugye's Third Letter to Yulgok

10.9b   I am truly delighted to learn about the excellent state of your affairs from your letters. I have already attentively read three times the separate sheets that arrived yesterday.

In regard to T'oegye's explanations, I have always felt that there was something not entirely clear, but every time I read Kobong's argument, it seemed perfectly clear and indubitable. But recently I have been reading Master Chu's explanation regarding the human mind and the Tao mind [in his preface to the *Doctrine of the Mean*]: Its thesis that "the one arises [from the individuality (*ssu*)[1] of the psychophysical endowment] while the other originates [in the correctness of the normative nature]" seems to tally with T'oegye's position. Therefore, I was struck to think that even in the time of Yao and Shun, when there was not much theorizing, there was this thesis regarding the mutual issuance of principle and material force; so it seems that Master T'oegye's view is a position that should not be changed. On the contrary, I am inclined to discard my former views and accept it.

Therefore, I venture to put the question to you. With regard to the rationale of the human mind/Tao mind and Four [Beginnings]/Seven [Feelings] terminology, I have no desire to make a forced comparison and equate them, straining the one to fit with the other. Any attempt to summarize the boundless truths taught by the sages and worthies in a single statement or to treat them uniformly and make sweeping comparisons would be like being presented with a wide variety of dishes and chewing them up together in a single mouthful: Not only would one not recognize the flavor, one would also miss discerning the proper sourness, sweetness, saltiness, or bitterness appropriate to each.

10.10a   I am raising the question out of a desire to know whether the meaning and intent of the Four and Seven and the human mind and Tao mind are the same or not, so as to see whether or not the thesis regarding the mutual issuance of principle and material force is compatible with them. Generally speaking, although there is some difference in what was meant in setting up the theories of the Four and Seven and the human mind and Tao mind, they are both explanations of the function of the nature and the feelings, that is all. But then if the mutual issuance of principle and material force thesis were not one of the world's fixed principles, how could Master Chu have spoken in this way?

This explanation is too long, and my grasp of it is not entirely clear. I have already entered the midst of the complexities of the argument between Kobong and Master T'oegye, so how can I simply solve it for myself through your letter? As in the case of Kobong, it's not that your explanation is not perfectly clear and to the point, but that I have some question as to whether the truth might be like this [i.e., like T'oegye's theory], that is all. So I wish again to deeply inquire into and continually give exacting thought to the purport of the "the one arises . . . the other originates"[2] passage. If, after continuing in this practice, I attain something, I shall quickly let you know.

What I meant [in my earlier letter] was that if the human mind and Tao mind are expressions that have to do with the issuance of the mind, that is dissimilar from what is signified by the category **10.10b**   of the Four and Seven, which has to do with the issuance of the nature, that is all. I did not mean to say that the human mind and the Tao mind are just issued by the mind and do not have anything to do with the nature and the feelings. What you expressed in your letter as their combining both feelings and intention is really just what I meant in saying they were dissimilar; but in my case I was not able to enunciate it fully, that is all.

This is the cornerstone of the foundation for truth; if one makes a mistake here, everything will be mistaken. We must truly be absolutely resolved; our investigation must eventuate in the truth. I have recently vomited blood and feel very unwell; thus my words cannot adequately express what I really wish to say, and I beg leave to communicate it to you later.

Kobong's explanation of the Four and Seven says: "In discussing the human mind and the Tao mind perhaps one may use such an explanation, but when it comes to the Four Beginnings and the Seven Feelings, I suspect one may not explain it in such fashion" [A2a]. In my humble opinion, if one may use this explanation in discussion of the human mind and the Tao mind, then one can use it as well in discussing the Four Beginnings and Seven Feelings. Why is it that one may not use this explanation? About this point I wish you to give me a solution and discussion that brings us back to agreement. This I most earnestly pray!

I think that if one may distinguish and speak of the predominance of principle or the predominance of material force with regard to the nature, then when it comes to the issuance as feelings, how is it that there is no difference regarding the predominance of principle or the predominance of material force? I would be most happy if you could enlighten me on this point as well.

CHAPTER 13

Yulgok's Response to Ugye's Third Letter

> *Yulgok's response to Ugye's letter is a tour de force that illustrates the brilliance and clarity of exposition that earned him an unprecedented first ranking in nine successive levels of the civil service examinations. His review of the relationship of principle and material force in the dualistic monism of Ch'eng-Chu metaphysics achieves a scope, precision, and clarity rare in Neo-Confucian literature. He follows this with an excellent exposition of the human mind and Tao mind and the relationship of the Four Beginnings and Seven Feelings. His ability to distill convincing clarity and consistency from the tensions inherent in the disparate sources incorporated into Chu Hsi's great synthesis make his one of the most forceful and persuasive philosophical elaborations of Ch'eng-Chu thought.*

10.2a   How have things been going for you these days? In my last letter to you, explaining the mind, nature, and feelings, I thought I had been quite exact and exhaustive, but now that I have received your letter I find that there are many points that do not add up. It is disappointing that after repeatedly [going over this], you still have not broken through. It is twenty years since you set your resolve on the pursuit of learning, and it's not that you have not read the writings of the sages and worthies. And yet you still do not have a solid understanding of the mind, nature, and feelings; I suspect that this is because there is yet something you have not grasped about the two terms, principle and material force. Now I would like to discuss them; I hope you will not reject it.

In general, principle is the master of material force, and material force is what principle mounts upon. Without principle, material force has no grounding; without material force, principle has nothing on which to depend. They are not two [separate] things, but again they are not a single thing. They are not a single thing, therefore they are one and yet two; they are not two things, therefore they are two and yet one.

What does it mean when I say they are not a single thing? Although principle and material force cannot be separated from one another, in the midst of their marvelous unity principle is principle and material force is material force; they never become intermingled and therefore are not as a single thing. What does it mean to say that they are not two things? Although one says principle is principle and material force is material force, they are interfused with no interstice, no anterior or posterior, no separating or conjoining; one does not perceive them as two [independent] things. Therefore, they are not two things, and so movement and rest have no distinct terminus, yin and yang do not have a beginning. Principle has no beginning, and therefore material force likewise has no beginning.

10.2b

Indeed, principle is one, and that is all. In it, there is originally no differentiation into the partial and the fully correct, the penetrating and the blocked up, the clear and the turbid, the pure and the mixed. But the material force on which it is mounted rises and falls and flies about unceasingly, becoming mixed and variegated with numerous differences. It gives birth to Heaven and Earth and the myriad creatures, some of which are whole and some partial, some penetrating and some blocked up, some clear and some turbid, some pure and some mixed. Although principle is one, since it is mounted on material force it is differentiated in innumerable ways. Therefore, in Heaven and Earth it is the principle of Heaven and Earth, in the myriad creatures it is the principle of the myriad creatures, and in us humans it is the principle of us humans.

That being the case, the variation and lack of uniformity is the product of material force. But although one may say it is the product of material force, there must be principle as its master, so that whereby it becomes varied and lacking in uniformity is likewise a matter of principle that dictates that it ought to be like that. It's not that principle is not like that, but that material force alone is that way.

10.3a   Although Heaven and Earth, men, and other creatures each have their own principle, the principle of Heaven and Earth is the principle of the myriad creatures, and the principle of the myriad creatures is the principle of us humans. This is what is described as the unified substance "being the one Supreme Ultimate."[1] Although one says it is the one principle, the nature of man is not the nature of other creatures, and the dog's nature is not the nature of a cow. This is what is described as "each has its single nature."[2]

If one considers the foundation of this, principle and material force are the father and mother of Heaven and Earth, and again Heaven and Earth are the father and mother of men and other creatures. Since Heaven and Earth have obtained the perfectly whole and perfectly penetrating material force, they therefore have a fixed nature that does not change. The myriad creatures have received partial and blocked up material force, so they likewise have fixed natures that do not change. Therefore, Heaven and Earth and the myriad creatures can never have techniques for the practice of self-cultivation.

Only human beings have received integral and penetrating material force and at the same time have innumerable variations as to the degree of clarity or turbidity, being pure or mixed. They do not have the pure uniformity of Heaven and Earth; but the mind-and-heart, being empty, spiritual, and penetrating, is fully endowed with the myriad principles. Thus the turbid can change and become clear, the mixed can change and become pure. Therefore the practice of self-cultivation belongs only to man, and the ultimate perfection of that practice extends even to bringing it about that Heaven and Earth assume their proper positions and all creatures are properly nurtured.[3] Only then is the service that is within the human capacity fulfilled.

10.3b   Among human beings, there are sages. They alone have received perfectly penetrating and perfectly integral, perfectly clear and perfectly pure material force, and so they are at one with the character of Heaven and Earth. Therefore, the sage likewise has a fixed nature that does not change. Only after one has a fixed nature that does not change can he be said to have "fulfilled his bodily design."[4] That being the case, Heaven and Earth are the norm for the sage, and the sage is the norm for the ordinary man. That which is termed techniques of self-cultivation are nothing more than a matter of following the norms that have already been formulated by the sages, that is all.

In the case of other creatures, however, their natures are not able to embody the integral character [of Heaven and Earth], their minds-and-hearts are not able to penetrate all principles. And as for plants and trees that are completely blocked up, they certainly are hardly worth mention. But the birds and beasts may perchance penetrate one aspect or another. There is, for example, the father-son relationship among tigers and wolves, bees and ants have the ruler-subject relationship, the marching of geese shows the order between elder and younger brothers, doves and pigeons have the proper distinction between husband and wife; those that dwell in nests or underground have the wisdom of premonition, and seasonal insects are faithful in awaiting their proper time. But none of these is capable of changing and adapting. They each realize their natures only because man participates in the transformative and nurturing process [of Heaven and Earth], that is all.

For man has received the directive principle of Heaven and Earth as his nature and has been allotted what fills up all between Heaven and Earth as his body.[5] Therefore, the function of our minds-and-hearts is identical with the transformative process of Heaven and Earth.

10.4a   The transformative process of Heaven and Earth does not have two roots; therefore, neither does the issuance of our minds-and-hearts have two origins.

Conscious consistency with the cosmic metaphysical framework is a noteworthy element in Yulgok's handling of the entire question of principle and material force in the realm of human psychology and morality. A Western thinker, steeped in traditions that make man discontinuous from nature, would quickly observe that principle as natural law and principle as moral norm are not exactly the same thing, and that the turbidity of material force as an explanation for different species is not the same as the turbidity of material force as an explanation for moral differences, but Neo-Confucian thought does not make such distinctions. In its close juxtaposition of cosmic and moral discourses concerning principle and material force, the Four-Seven Debate tests the resources of the tradition. The challenge is, can Yulgok be consistent and still achieve as adequate a treatment of the psychological and moral sphere as could T'oegye, for whom adequacy to the human phenomenon took precedence over all.

"Man's being quiet at birth is the nature given him by Heaven; his being stimulated by things and moving is a matter of the desires of his nature."[6] When stimulated and moved, one desires to dwell in humanity, one desires to proceed with righteousness, one wants to return to propriety, one desires to investigate principle, one wishes to be loyal and faithful, one desires to be filial to his parents, one desires to be loyal to his ruler, one wishes to rectify his household, to be reverent to his elder brother and to be trustworthy to friends. These sorts of things are described as the "Tao mind." Being stimulated and moving is certainly a matter of the psychophysical constitution, but its issuance emerges directly from the integrity of humanity, righteousness, propriety, and wisdom, and is not disrupted or distorted by the psychophysical constitution. Therefore, the predominant thing is principle, and [such desires] are categorized as Tao mind.

But if one is hungry, he wants food; if cold, he desires clothes; if thirsty, he desires drink; if he itches, he wants to scratch; the eyes desire colors, the ears sounds, and the four limbs desire comfort. These sorts of things are described as the "human mind." Although their origin is rooted in the nature given by Heaven, their issuance proceeds from the individual particularity of one's eyes, ears, and limbs. [Such desires] are not the normative principle in its original condition; therefore, the predominant thing is material force, and they are categorized as the human mind.

The issuance of the Tao mind is like a fire beginning to burn or a spring just issuing forth, insofar as at first they are difficult to see; hence it is described as "subtle." The issuance of the human

10.4b   mind is like a hawk loosed from its tether or a horse that has slipped its bridle, insofar as their flying or galloping off is hard to control; hence it is described as "perilous."[7] Although the human mind and the Tao mind bear two different names, their origin is just the one mind-and-heart. As for its issuances, some have to do with principle and righteousness, while others have to do with food and sex. Therefore, following the nature of the issuances, they have been given different names.

But in the case of the mutual issuance of principle and material force as you spoke of it in your letter, principle and material force would be two separate things, each with its roots within our minds. Even before [the mind-and-heart] is aroused, there would already be the incipient shoots of the human mind and Tao mind: if principle gives issue then it is the Tao mind; if material force gives issue then it is the human mind. In that case, our mind-and-heart would have two roots. Wouldn't that be a great error? Master Chu said, "The emptiness, spirituality and consciousness of the mind-and-heart are one and that is all."[8] Whence did you ever get this mutual issuance of principle and material force theory? [Master Chu's] speaking of the one as being originated [from principle] and the other as arising [from material force] was a proposition dealing with the condition when issuance has taken place. When the issuance has to do with principle and righteousness, then he searched for its cause by asking whence we have these dispositions toward principle and righteousness. They proceed from the normative nature in the mind-and-heart; therefore we have this "Tao mind." When the issuance has to do with food and sex, he searched for its cause by asking whence we have this inclination toward food and sex. It proceeds from the vital forces that constitute our physical being; therefore, we have this "human mind."

10.5a   That's all he said. It is nothing like the mutual issuance thesis, with principle sometimes giving issuance, and material force sometimes giving issuance, and the Great Foundation losing its unity.

> *Yulgok's discussion of the reasoning process leading to the association of principle and material force with the Tao mind and human mind is verbally very similar to the one that T'oegye used*

in his argument that the Four Beginnings and Seven Feelings have different points of origin (A39a). But T'oegye insists this be understood in terms of some real causal distinction (A43b), while for Yulgok it is only a matter of analytic reference to factors in the human composite having to do with the norm and variance from the norm. His whole point is to deny the causal distinction he sees embodied in the phrase "mutual issuance."

Generally speaking, that which gives issuance is material force; that whereby there is issuance is principle. Without material force, there would not be the power of issuing; without principle, there would not be that whereby it issues. (*Even though a sage should be born again, the words from "that which gives issuance" on could not be changed.*) "Having no priority and posteriority" and "having no separation and conjunction" could not apply to mutual issuance.

It's just that in the case of the human mind and the Tao mind, the one has to do with the psychophysical constitution and the other has to do with morality. Although the origin is the same, its outflow branches so that certainly one cannot but explain it as split into two. But such is not the case when it comes to the Four Beginnings and Seven Feelings. The Four Beginnings are the good side of the Seven Feelings, and the Seven Feelings are a comprehensive term that includes the Four Beginnings. How can one take [the term representing] one side and the comprehensive term and turn them into a dichotomy in which they stand in contrast to each other?

Master Chu's thesis regarding an issuing by principle and an issuing by material force certainly had a point, but nowadays people just hang on to the thesis without understanding its point. Since they analyze it and distort it so, how could the result be anything but turning it over and over and losing its true meaning? Master Chu's point indeed was nothing more than saying that the Four Beginnings refer exclusively to principle, while the Seven Feelings refer inclusively to material force. That's all he was saying. He was not saying that, in the case of the Four Beginnings, principle first gives issue and, in the case of the Seven Feelings, material force first gives issue.

10.5b   T'oegye based himself on these [words of Chu Hsi] and established a theory that said: "In the case of the Four Beginnings, principle gives issue and material force follows it; in the case of the Seven Feelings, material force gives issue and principle mounts it" [cf. A40a]. What he says about material force giving issue and principle mounting it is permissible. But this is not the case only with the Seven Feelings; the Four Beginnings are likewise a case of material force giving issue and principle mounting it. What do I mean? Only after seeing the child about to fall into the well is there the issuance of feelings of commiseration. Seeing it and feeling commiseration has to do with material force; this is what is described as material force giving issue. The root of commiseration is humanity; this is what is described as principle mounting it.

It is not only in the case of the mind-and-heart of man that this is so; the transformative process of Heaven and Earth is completely a matter of material force transforming and principle mounting it. Therefore yin and yang cycle in rest and movement, and the Supreme Ultimate mounts it. Here there is no priority or posteriority to speak of. But when it comes to the thesis that principle gives issue and material force follows it, then clearly there is priority and posteriority. Does this not do violence to the truth?

Heaven and Earth's [natural] process of transformation is identical with the issuing of our minds-and-hearts. If, in the transformative process of Heaven and Earth, there are cases in which principle transforms and cases in which material force transforms, then in our minds-and-hearts there likewise should be cases in which principle gives issuance and material force gives issuance. But since Heaven and Earth do not differentiate between principle transforming and material force transforming, how can there be a difference between principle giving issuance and material force giving issuance in the case of our minds-and-hearts? If someone were to say that our minds-and-hearts are different from the transformative process of Heaven and Earth, that's not something I
10.6a   could understand. *(This section is most important for you to understand. If we do not agree on this, then I fear there is no hope for our final agreement.)*

Moreover, the statement regarding being issued by principle is like saying that the nature issues forth as the feelings. But if one says principle gives issuance and material force follows it, that means that at the very first moment of issuance, material force is not involved, but rather after that issuance it follows and gives issue. Is this reasonable?

The discussion by T'oegye and Ki Myŏngŏn [Kobong] of the Four-Seven thesis runs to more than ten thousand words. Myŏngŏn's discussion is clear and straightforward, with the kind of force it takes to crush bamboos. But in T'oegye's case, although his argumentation is precise, the meaning is not clear, and one chews it over repeatedly without getting the taste of reality in it. One could not venture to put Myŏngŏn's learning on a par with that of T'oegye. It's just that he had a particular aptitude for arriving at a thorough understanding of this matter, that's all.

I take T'oegye's meaning to be that the Four Beginnings proceed from within and issue, while the Seven Feelings are stimulated externally and issue. With this as his preconception, he asserted it in terms of Master Chu's statement regarding being issued by principle and being issued by material force and further elaborated it, causing considerable controversy. Every time I read it I cannot help sighing, for this is the one imperfection in his otherwise accurate grasp [of this point].

The *Book of Changes* says, "It is still and unmoving; when it is stimulated, it goes forth and penetrates [all things]."[9] [As we see in this description,] even the mind-and-heart of a sage has never moved of itself with no stimulus. There must be a stimulus for it to move, and that which does the stimulating is always some external thing.

10.6b

What do I mean by this? With the father as stimulus, there is the movement of filial piety, with the ruler as stimulus, there is the movement of loyalty, with the elder brother as stimulus, there is the movement of reverence. How could the father, the ruler, or the elder brother be considered principles residing within [the mind-and-heart]?! How in the world could there be feelings that proceed from within and issue of themselves with no stimulus?

But since that by which [the mind-and-heart] is stimulated

includes both right and wrong things and its movement is subject to excess and deficiency, there is a distinction between good and evil, that is all. Now if one regards the Four Beginnings as something that proceeds from within and issues of itself without awaiting an external stimulus, that would amount to filial piety issuing with no father, loyalty issuing with no ruler, reverence issuing with no elder brother. How could this be the true nature of man's feelings! To take the example of commiseration [in *Mencius*], after seeing the child about to fall into the well, this disposition issues forth. That by which it is stimulated is the child, and is not the child an external thing? How could there be a case of commiseration issuing of itself with no child about to fall into a well? Even if one conceded that there might be such a case, it would be nothing more than a type of mental illness, that's all. It could not be [normal] human feelings.

Human nature is constituted of humanity, righteousness, propriety, wisdom, and fidelity—these five and that is all. Beyond these five, there is no other human nature. The feelings comprise pleasure, anger, sorrow, fear, love, hatred, and desire—these seven and that is all. Beyond these seven, there are no other feelings. The Four Beginnings are just alternative terms for the good feelings; if one says "the Seven Feelings," the Four Beginnings are included in them. It is nothing like the case of the human mind and Tao mind, which are terms set up to contrast with each other. Why do you insist on pairing them up and treating them as comparable?

10.7a

In general, the human mind and Tao mind are terms set up in contrast with each other. When one says "Tao mind," the human mind is excluded; when one says "human mind," the Tao mind is excluded. Therefore, one can explain them dichotomously. But when it comes to the Seven Feelings, they already include the Four Beginnings. One cannot say that the Four Beginnings are not the Seven Feelings, or that the Seven Feelings are not the Four Beginnings. How could one make a dichotomous division of them! Have you not yet realized that the Seven Feelings include the Four Beginnings?

For in the case of human feelings, when one meets with

something pleasant, he feels pleasure; when one is involved with mourning, he feels sorrow; when one sees one's intimates, he feels tender affection; when one sees principle, he desires to investigate it; and when one sees a wise man, he wants to emulate him. *(The above represent the four feelings of pleasure, sorrow, love, and desire.)*[10] They are the manifestations *(tan)*[11] of humanity. Meeting with something provocative and becoming angry, or meeting something evil and hating it *(the two feelings of anger and hatred)* are the manifestations of righteousness. Seeing someone of honor and eminence and feeling awed *(the feeling of fear)* is a manifestation of propriety. Encountering occasions of pleasure, anger, sorrow, or fear, and understanding that one should feel pleasure, should be angry, should feel sorrow, or should feel fear *(These all belong to the class of what is right)* or again understanding that one should not feel pleasure, one should not become angry, one

10.7b should not feel sorrow, one should not fear *(These belong to the class of what is wrong. In these cases [the sense of right and wrong, which belongs to the Four Beginnings] is conjoined with the Seven Feelings as the understanding of their righteousness or wrongness)* that this is the manifestation of wisdom. The issuance of the good feelings cannot be completely enumerated, but they are roughly like this.

If one were to match the Four Beginnings with the Seven Feelings, commiseration belongs with love, the sense of shame and dislike belongs with hatred, modesty and reverence belong with fear, and the sense of right and wrong belongs with the feeling of understanding whether or not one should feel pleasure, anger, and so on. Outside the Seven Feelings, there are no other Four Beginnings. That being the case, the Four Beginnings selectively refer to the Tao mind, while the Seven Feelings combine both the human mind and the Tao mind. Is this not far different from the way the human mind and Tao mind divide dichotomously?

As for your thesis [cf. 10.10b] regarding the nature that [one may differentiate in terms of] a particular focus on principle or a particular focus on material force, although it seems harmless, I fear that it harbors within it the roots of further problems. The "original nature" refers exclusively to principle and does not touch on material force. The "psychophysical nature" inclusively refers to material force that enfolds principle within it. So, in this case likewise, one cannot generalize with a dichotomous division that explains it in terms of a particular focus on principle or a particular focus on material force. If one makes a dichotomy of the original nature and the psychophysical nature, will not the ignorant conclude that there are two natures?

10.8a   Moreover, in the case of the Four Beginnings, it is permissible to characterize them in terms of a particular focus on principle; but it is wrong to characterize the Seven Feelings as having a particular focus on material force. The Seven Feelings refer inclusively to both principle and material force; they are not a matter of a particular focus on material force. (*In the case of the human mind and Tao mind one can make an explanation in terms of the predominance of principle or the predominance of material force. But one cannot use such an explanation for the Four Beginnings and Seven Feelings because the Four Beginnings are included in the Seven Feelings, and the Seven Feelings include both principle and material force.*) When Tzu Ssu was discussing the character of the nature and the feelings he said: "Before the feelings of pleasure, anger, sorrow, and joy are aroused, it is called equilibrium; when these feelings are aroused and each attains perfect measure, it is called harmony."[12] Here he mentions only the Seven Feelings and does not mention the Four Beginnings. If, as according to you, the Seven Feelings are a matter of the predominance of material force, then Tzu Ssu would be discussing the Great Foundation and Universal Path and neglecting to mention the side that is principle! Would that not be a great error?!

Moral truth is vast, and establishing adequate propositions is exceedingly difficult. Although there may be nothing wrong with one's words, when readers are hindered by the personal inclinations, they carry in their minds and force [the words] to fit, there is always a serious problem. Thus there are even cases in which later scholars have been misled by the words of the ancient sages and wise men. Master Ch'eng said: "The [concrete] implement is also the Tao; the Tao is also the [concrete] implement."[13] Here he was stating that principle and material force cannot be separated, but readers concluded that principle and material force are a single thing. Master Chu said: "Principle and material force are definitely two things."[14] Here he was stating that principle and material force do not become mixed together, but readers concluded that principle and material force have priority and posteriority. The recent **10.8b** propositions on the so-called question of whether the nature or the mind moves first are certainly hardly worth mentioning. But even a man of Lo Cheng-an's lofty intelligence and sophistication also had a slight problem regarding taking principle and material force as a single thing.[15] And even though there is nowadays no match for the exactness and careful precision of T'oegye, his thesis that "principle gives issue and material force follows it" likewise had a slight problem regarding principle and material force having priority and posteriority. While the old master was yet alive, I heard this thesis and knew the mistake, but at the time I was still young and my studies were too immature, so I did not venture to ask about the problem and seek a resolution. Every time I recall this, I painfully regret it.

In the past when we discussed principle and material force, your views were no different from mine. I was happy to think that although one might not be able to say that we two had a true view of the Great Foundation one could at least say that we recognized the meaning of the terms. But now I have received your letter, in which you are inclining toward accepting the mistake of taking principle and material force as two distinct branches; is this not a case of going wrong by trying to count the number of pillars in the colonnade yet again? How could your view be so unsettled? After you say that the discussion of Myŏngŏn and myself are clear and straightforward, you go on to doubt whether the truth is actually like that. That I find quite incomprehensible. Of the two theses, if one is right, the other is wrong; you cannot admit both and maintain them together. If the truth can at once be one way and then **10.9a** again another, that amounts to saying that the sweet can also be called the bitter and the white can also be called the black. How would there be any determined proposition in the whole world?

If you do not trust my word, then repeatedly and carefully

mull over the *Reflections on Things at Hand*, the *Letter on Settling the Nature*,[16] and the section on "what one has at birth is called the nature."[17] Then perhaps you will come to understand it. Truly, as your letter puts it, this matter involves the very foundations and great fountainhead of truth; if one makes a mistake here then he will not understand the Great Foundation. And then what is left to do?

If there is nothing for it but to take the human mind and Tao mind as your topic, with the inclination to focus on the thesis that principle and material force mutually give issuance, it would be better to go along with Lo Cheng-an in regarding the human mind and Tao mind as substance and function: although it mistakes the meaning of the terms, at least it does not amount to a serious error with regard to the Great Foundation. What do you think?

The anxious bunch in the world nowadays are not such as could be suddenly talked to about these matters, so you and I are together on a quiet and solitary shore: we cannot just each [separately] have regard for what he has gotten and each practice according to his understanding. Therefore, I have anxiously tried to resolve the matter without realizing it was all pouring out of me like this! I beg you to understand my wild presumptuousness, and will be most happy if you give this matter a leisurely inquiry with deep reflection.

CHAPTER 14

Ugye's Fourth Letter to Yulgok

> *In this letter, Ugye reintroduces the horse and rider image,*
> *using it to probe the Tao mind/human mind distinction much as*
> *T'oegye and Kobong used it with reference to the Four Begin-*
> *nings and Seven Feelings. The simile will be recalled repeatedly*
> *throughout the rest of this correspondence. Horse and rider rep-*
> *resent sources of potentially diverse tendencies, making a partic-*
> *ularly apt probe with which to push Yulgok's resolute insistence*
> *on a single absolutely interdependent mode in the* li-ki *relation-*
> *ship.*

0.18a   I received your last letter and was greatly delighted to learn that things are going well for you. I have caused you much trouble in writing such a long letter for my guidance, and am deeply indebted to you. The meaning of your words is lucid and the reasoning straightforward. When I read it over, it comes close to bestowing light on my darkness. But it's not only that. In your sorrow for my misunderstanding, you have instructed me with the most profound sincerity, as if fearing that your words might be incomplete; you have spared no efforts and gone to such great lengths on my behalf, I can hardly admire enough your diligence in giving guidance to others and your sincere compassionate intention to render mutual assistance. I am profoundly moved.

0.18b   Your last two letters both have the same purport. This matter was among the subjects we already discussed together in the past; could I venture to but reverently accept it? With respect to Master T'oegye, I have had a fascination with him. Every time I take up his thesis regarding principle and material force mutually giving

139

issue, I do not regard it as right, but it sticks in my mind and I cannot get rid of it. Then when I was reading [Chu Hsi's] explanation of the human mind and Tao mind and saw in front of me the statement that the one arises [from material force], while the other originates [from principle],[1] it implicitly coincided with what T'oegye said. Therefore, I was strongly attracted to it and wished to reject my former position and accept it. This is what caused me to change my mind.

The mutual issuance thesis is not my new creation, but, rather, the explanation given by the old master [i.e., T'oegye]. Now I beg to present a copy of his original text for your inspection. What the master had personally attained is in this section, and herein likewise is his correctness or his error.

When it comes to the explanation of the human mind and the Tao mind, I cannot but have some doubts. The ancients' comparison of principle mounting on material force and proceeding to act with a man coming and going mounted on a horse is truly good.[2] For without the horse, the man does not come or go, and without the man, the horse will lose the proper path: they are interdependent and inseparable. But when the man and horse go out, it must be at the wish of the man, and the horse awaits it. This is truly like principle being the master of material force, and material force being mounted by its principle. When they go forth, and the man and horse proceed by the proper path, it is an issuing forth with material force submissive to principle. But when even though the man is mounted on the horse, it gallops off the wrong way instead of proceeding by the proper path—this is like material force running wild and being either excessive or deficient. In this example, then, one can find the divergence of the subtle incipience of sincerity or of evil as principle and material force proceed with activity. Is this not clear and straightforward? And the rationale of the substance-function relationship between the nature and the feelings can be seen so clearly that one will not be lured by any deviant path.

A person's discernment of principle happens only after [the mind-and-heart] is aroused, whence good and evil are differentiated, and one then pronounces: "This is the issuance of the nature

10.19a

and is perfectly good," or "This sort of thing is a matter of the unevenness of material force and is devolving toward evil." Thinking it over in these terms, it's just that as soon as [the mind-and-heart] moves, at that very moment there is a difference of the predominance of principle or the predominance of material force. It's not that originally there is a mutual issuing with each taking control. A person's seeing it as a matter of principle or of material force is in each case a pronouncement based on the movement. Working it out like this, there is no contradiction with what you have said.

0.19b   How is it that Master Chu said: "The one arises from the individual particularity of the psychophysical constitution, while the other originates from the correctness of the normative nature"?[3] How is it that Ch'en Pei-hsi's explanation, "This is a matter of consciousness having issuances following from principle and issuances following from material force,"[4] is just like T'oegye's mutual issuance thesis?

That the Four and the Seven stand in contrast to each other and belong to distinct categories is certain. The human mind and the Tao mind are likewise a matter of feelings, so how is it that the Tao mind is regarded as principle giving issuance and the human mind is regarded as material force giving issuance? Human beings have this psychophysical constitution; in general, it means that the whole body and the mind-and-heart, and the particulars include all the hundred joints, and for every bit of it, there is a proper norm. Desires for sounds and colors and smells and tastes likewise issue from the unchangeableness of Heavenly Principle. Now if one says that one should restrict excess and properly moderate one's feelings, that is certainly a permissible sort of instruction. How is it that only the desires of the ears, the eye, the mouth, and the nose are categorized as matters of material force and called the human mind? Is it not that this material force also has occasions when it acts and functions of itself as a separate occurrence? If not, then why do you explain them in terms of material force? When a rider mounts a horse, they are interdependent in their going. And then if

0.20a   one points to the man as the Tao mind and to the horse as the human mind, it does not make sense, and likewise I do not understand where there is any real premise for referring distinctly to a human mind and a Tao mind.

If you will go over this section thoroughly and repeatedly and lay bare its meaning, once again instructing me on it, then if we break through at this juncture, everything else will tally. Generally speaking, as for pressing urgently on for reaching an agreement, how can one force it? It must wait upon meditative pondering and reflective examination, until one morning there will be the insight, and it will all be solved. Then finally the scattered pieces will come together again.

Of late, I have had guests come one after another, so I just hastily wrote this down, and the words do not quite catch my meaning. I beg that you will generously try to see what I am really trying to say and pray most earnestly that you will enlighten me on this matter.

T'oegye's original text says:

10.20b

I would say that considering the case of Heaven and Earth and man and other creatures likewise is not a matter of principle being outside of material force. If one can make the distinction in that case, then in the case of the nature or of the feelings, although one says that principle is in material force or the nature is in the psychophysical endowment, why is it impermissible to distinguish them? For in man's single body principle and material force combine and so he is born. Therefore the two mutually have an issuing function and moreover in the issuing they are interdependent. Since it is a mutual issuance one can see that each may have its particular role; they are interdependent, so one can see that both are included [in the issuing]. Since both are included, there is certainly an undifferentiated way of speaking of them; since each has its particular role, therefore there is nothing impermissible in a way of speaking that distinguishes them.

In discussing the nature, it is a situation of principle being in the midst of material force. If [in that situation] Tzu Ssu and Mencius could point out the original nature and the Ch'engs and Chang Tsai could single out for discussion the physical nature, then in discussing the feelings, a situation in which the nature is in the midst of the psychophysical endowment, why in that case alone should it be impermissible to consider in each case whence it issues and so distinguish the Four Beginnings and Seven Feelings in terms of their point of origin? The matter of combining principle and material force and having both good and evil does not pertain only to the feelings: the nature also is like that. How can you take this as evidence that it is not permissible to distinguish them? [A39a–b] (*From the point of view of principle being in material force, he argues that the nature is also [similar to the feelings] in that respect.*)

0.21a   With reference to the time after man is born with his physical form, the nature in the not-yet-aroused condition [of the mind-and-heart] (*speaking of it together with the psychophysical component*) must have a determination of good and evil. That being so, one may not describe it as the condition of equilibrium before [the mind-and-heart] is aroused. What I call "the substance in the not-yet-aroused condition" refers to the psychophysical endowment in its determinate condition. It does not refer to the equilibrium of the not-yet-aroused condition. The two phrases [in the above T'oegye passage] "It does not pertain only to the feelings; the nature also is like that" are just like what I am trying to get at. What you say in your letter about not being able to speak of evil with reference to the equilibrium that belongs to the not-yet-aroused condition is perfectly true. My words were without substance or foundation, just something I came up with.[5]

Yesterday I went out by Willow Stream; I splashed the water with my hand and then thought about it as follows: The water's flowing downward is a matter of principle; when it comes to splashing it, it's up in my hand—that is a matter of material force. In that case, are there occasions when material force functions and occasions when there is a mutual issuing? A certain Mr. Lee committed great crimes and was extremely evil, but to the end, he kept his life intact. Was it likewise perhaps because of actions of material force that the Tao of Heaven was unaware of this? And then I had another thought: what is done by material force is not determined and does not have principle as its master, then by now the sun and moon would have no brightness and Heaven and Earth would long ago have collapsed. Is that not an error? I thought it over without being able to decide the issue, and laughed at myself and returned home. Perhaps it will give you a smile. What about it?

CHAPTER 15

Yulgok's Reply to Ugye's Fourth Letter

> *In this response, Yulgok insists that "there is a single thread running through both the explanation of principle and material force and the explanation of the human mind and the Tao mind." He explores the interdependence of principle and material force in various levels of moral functioning or malfunctioning using the images of a pitcher and water and of the horse and rider.*

0.11a As soon as I received your letter, I looked to see how you are doing and was encouraged to find that you are well. Things are alright here. I am moved at how upset you are, and knowing that you are about to have a breakthrough, I have not hesitated to be somewhat repetitious in trying to present my humble views thoroughly. What great good fortune that rather than being rejected, the gist [of my argument] has met with your acceptance.

In a case like this, it does not take an extraordinary brilliance to see the true principle of the matter. Even though one's endowment may not be the most lofty and penetrating, if one accumulates the effects of continuous sincerity and applies himself, what principle is there that he cannot understand! The bright person understands it easily, but, on the contrary, may not be able to be vigorous in practicing it in order to fulfill what he sees. One who has accumulated the effects of continuous sincerity, because of the depth of his application, once he has understood something will find the vigorous practice of it easy. This is what I would expect in your case.

There is a single thread running through the explanations of both principle and material force and the human mind and the Tao mind. If one has not comprehended the meaning of the human mind and the Tao mind, it amounts to not comprehending principle and material force. If one has already clearly understood the inseparability of principle and material force, then one can extend that

10.11b   to an understanding of the fact that the human mind and Tao mind do not have a twofold origin. Only if there is something not yet comprehended about [the relationship of] principle and material force might one perhaps regard them as able to be separate, with each occupying its own distinct place. And thus one might also then question whether there might be two [distinct] origins in the case of the human mind and the Tao mind.

The treatment of your hesitations in my last letter was so precise in discernment and explication and the analogies so to the point [that I would have thought that] looking it over but once could bring agreement. But seeing that even then you still have doubts, it might be best to put the matter aside for a time and read extensively in the writings of the sages and worthies, and wait for understanding to come later. I myself got a glimpse of this matter already some ten years ago, and from then on little by little thought it out. Every time I read the classics and the commentaries, I always read one text in the light of the others. At first, there were times when things did not fit together, but afterward they gradually fell into place, and now it has all coalesced and fit together with a decisiveness that is beyond doubt. A hundred thousand most eloquent speakers could not change my understanding. I only regret that my psychophysical endowment is so coarse that I have not been up to vigorously putting it into practice and making it a reality, for which I continually sigh and reproach myself.

10.12a   Principle is above forms; material force is on the level of form. The two cannot be separated from each other. If they cannot be separated, then their issuance as function is single, and one cannot speak of them as mutually possessing issuing functions. If one says they mutually possess issuing functions, then that would mean that when principle issued as function material force at times might not be right with it, or that when material force issued as function there might be times when principle is not right with it. In that case, [the relation of] principle and material force would admit of both separation and conjunction and priority and posteriority. Activity and tranquillity would have a commencement; yin and yang would have a beginning. The error in all this is indeed anything but small!

But principle is non-active; rather, it is material force that has [concrete] activity. Therefore, in the case of feelings that emerge from the original nature and are not disrupted by our physical constitution, they are classed on the side of principle. Those that, although they initially emerge from the original nature, are then disrupted by the physical constitution and are classed on the side of material force. One cannot get by without such propositions. That which accounts for the original goodness of man's nature is principle, but if it were not for material force, principle, [being non-active], would have no issuance. Then as for the human mind and the Tao mind, are they not indeed both rooted in principle? It's not a matter of the systematic sprouts of the human mind already standing in contrast to principle in the mind-and-heart in the state before it is aroused. The wellspring is single, but its outpouring is dual; how could Master Chu not have understood this! It's just that the kinds of expressions used to clarify the matter for others each focuses on a predominant factor.

Master Ch'eng said, "It's not correct that good and evil are in **0.12b** the nature as two contrasting items that each has its own emergence."[1] Indeed, good and evil are two distinct things, but there is still no rationale whereby they stand in contrast [in the mind] and each emerge separately. How much more is this so in the case of principle and material force, which are inseparably intermixed; how could there be a rationale whereby they stand in contrast and mutually give issuance! If Master Chu actually thought that principle and material force have as function mutual issuances that could contrast with each other and each emerge on their own, then that would mean that Master Chu is also mistaken. But [one who could make such an error] could not be a Master Chu!

As for developing the terminology of "human mind" and "Tao mind," how did the sage have any alternative? Principle in its original condition is definitely perfectly good, but it mounts material force to issue as function, and this is where good and evil diverge. If one only sees that it mounts material force and involves both good and evil and does not understand principle in its original condition, then that amounts to not knowing the Great Foundation. If one only sees principle's original condition and does not understand its mounting on material force to issue as function—a condition that may devolve into evil—then that is like mistaking the bandit for a son. Therefore, the sage was concerned about this matter and categorized the feelings that directly follow from our normative nature in its original condition as the "Tao mind" in order to get people to preserve and nurture it and develop it to the fullest extent. The feelings that are disrupted by [the effects of] our physical constitution and are unable to be the direct consequence of our normative nature in its original condition he categorized as the "human mind" in order to get people to examine the excess or

10.13a deficiency involved in such feelings and moderate them accordingly.

> *In focusing on Tao mind and human mind, the analysis becomes one of normative versus potentially errant tendencies. The T'oegye-Kobong discussion pushed the question in the direction of why some feelings seem to be more inherently normative, while others are more questionable. Ugye also repeatedly introduces this angle (above, 10.19b, below, 10.23b), but within Yulgok's framework, there is no place for such a distinction: the variation in the turbidity of ki is the sole source of differentiation, and it encompasses the whole of the life of the mind-and-heart. Thus he is eloquent in explaining different degrees of moral perfection in terms of different psychophysical constitutions, but systematically skirts the question of whether some part of our emotional makeup is intrinsically more prone to lead us astray.*

That which moderates them is the Tao mind. Indeed, concrete form is a part of the nature with which we are endowed by Heaven, and as for the human mind, how is it likewise not good? [But its negative connotation] is from its involving excess or deficiency and devolving into evil, that is all. If one is able to develop the Tao mind to its fullest extent and moderate the human mind, making [the proclivities that attend] our physical constitution each follow their proper norm, then be it in activity or tranquillity, speech or deeds, there will be nothing that is not of our normative nature in its original condition.

From ancient times, this has been the main purport of the sages' and worthies' method of cultivating the mind-and-heart. But how is this in any way related to the theory of the mutual issuance of principle and material force? The problem with T'oegye is essentially a matter of just the two words "mutual issuance." How regrettable! Even with all the old master's subtlety and precision there was, as it were, a heavy membrane interposed with regard to the Great Foundation. As for the theory of Mister Ch'en Pei-hsi, I am not yet certain: did he also understand in what the intention of Master Chu consisted, or did he really hold the mutual issuance theory as T'oegye understands it? This matter we cannot ascertain, but the correct principle is definitely this way.

We need only to maintain this viewpoint, practice it with vigor, and make it a reality. We should not just question without settling anything, so that differences and similarities in our theories end up upsetting our minds. The Buddhists have a saying: "Although gold dust is valuable, if it falls in your eye, it blinds you." Following this analogy, although the explanations of the sages and worthies are valuable, if one misunderstands them, they become harmful.

10.13b   This is a very good saying! As regards the words and intentions of the sages and worthies, if someone is in the position of not seeking the intention and is just mired in the words, do they not on the contrary become harmful? For example, Confucius said, "Having lost one's post, what is called for is rapid impoverishment; as for the dead, what is called for is rapid decomposition."[2] Even such a one as Tseng Tzu still regarded these words as proper. If it were not for the discernment of Yu Tzu, throughout later ages, households of those who lost their posts would have had to throw out their provisions and get rid of their money, and those who send off their dead would have had to regard a minimal burial as proper.[3] But how could this have been the sage's intent!

As for Master Chu's explanation that the one has its origin in principle and the other arises through material force, in a similar manner we must seek out his intent and grasp it, not get mired in the words and try to assert a thesis that there is a mutual issuance. Of the Confucians of recent times, Lo Cheng-an stood out as the most knowledgeable and keen-minded. He knew something of the Great Foundation, but, on the contrary, he questioned whether Master Chu might have an [excessively] dualistic view; in this, although it was a misunderstanding of Master Chu, there was, however, an understanding as regards the Great Foundation. But his regarding the human mind and the Tao mind as a matter of substance and function was a misinterpretation of the meaning of the terms, and that likewise is regrettable. Nonetheless, Cheng-an's mistake was at the level of terminology, while T'oegye's mistake had to do with the nature and principle. T'oegye's error was thus far more grave. (*As for what is taken up in this section, one certainly could not just show it right off to others. Those who do not understand would certainly think I am criticizing T'oegye. When Sojae[4] was inclined to follow Cheng-an [Lo Chin-shun]'s position on the human mind and Tao mind, that likewise was because he thought the mutual issuance thesis was wrong. His view was fundamentally right, but the meaning of the human mind/Tao mind terminology can be understood without bringing in the mutual issuance question. What need is there for that? If I took this up with Sojae it seems likely he would agree, but the right opportunity has not come up so I have not ventured to ask him.*)

10.14a

As for something that cannot be separated from a vessel and has ceaseless activity, water is just the thing. Thus water is just the metaphor for principle. The original clarity of water is like the nature's original goodness. The difference between a clean and a dirty vessel is like the differentiation of the physical nature. When the vessel moves, the water moves, which is like material force issuing and principle mounting it. The vessel and the water move together; there is no difference between the vessel moving and the water moving. Nor is there a difference in the issuance of material force and principle, as suggested by the mutual issuance theory. When the vessel moves, the water necessarily moves; the water never moves itself. Principle is non-active; it is material force that has activity.

The psychophysical endowment of a sage is perfectly pure, and his nature is in integral possession of its substance without a single bit of the self-centeredness of selfish human desires. Therefore, as for the issuance of this nature, "he can follow his heart's desire without transgressing the norm,"[5] and the human mind is likewise the Tao mind. It's like a perfectly clean vessel filled with water: since there is not a speck of dirt, when it moves and the originally clear water is poured out and flows forth, it remains entirely clear water.

0.14b   As for the worthy, although his psychophysical endowment is pure, it has not escaped a slight admixture of turbidity. Therefore, it must be supplemented by the application of further cultivation before it regains the full perfection of the original nature. As for its issuance, there is that which is the direct consequence of the original nature and is not disrupted by the physical constitution. There is also that which, although it issues from the nature, is also affected by the physical constitution; but although the physical constitution has some effect, the human mind submits to what is mandated by the Tao mind. Therefore, the appetites for food and sex also stay on the right track. It is like a vessel filled with water that is basically clean, but has not escaped a slight bit of dirt inside: there must be further cleansing before the water regains its original clarity. Therefore, as for its movement, sometimes there is clear water that pours out and the dirt has not yet moved. There are other cases when, although clean water comes out, the dirt has already been moved, so the dirt must be stopped and not allowed to become mixed in, and then the outpouring water can keep its clarity.

One who has no semblance [of his original perfection][6] has a psychophysical endowment that has a lot of the turbid and little of the clear in it, much that is impure and little that is pure. The original condition of the nature is overwhelmed, and, moreover, there is no application made to cultivate and perfect it. What issues forth in such a case is for the most part because of the physical constitution; here the human mind is in control. Intermittently, the Tao mind emerges mixed in with the human mind, but he does not know how to discern and preserve it, so he consistently gives himself over to the self-centered proclivity of his physical constitution.

10.15a	When this reaches the point of one's being conquered by the feelings, concupiscence burns hotly, and the Tao mind is reduced to the human mind. It is like an unclean, filthy vessel filled with water: the mud-filled water has lost its original clarity, and there is, moreover, no effort to cleanse it. As for its movement, muddy, roiled water comes forth, and one sees no evidence of its having been clean water. There are occasions when the mud has not yet been roiled up, and suddenly clear water comes out for a moment, but in the blink of an eye, the mud is again roiled up, so what was clear again becomes turbid, and what flows forth is all dirty water.

The nature is originally good, but the influence of the [imperfect] psychophysical endowment at times causes it to devolve into evil. Not to regard evil as the original condition of the nature is permissible; to say that it is not based on the nature is impermissible. The water is originally clear, but the roiling up of the mud makes it end up as a turbid outflow. One may regard the turbidity as not the original condition of water, but one cannot say that the [turbid] outflow is not that of water.[7]

The middle sort of person's nature falls between that of the worthy and the person who bears no semblance [to his original condition]. One can understand it by following it out along these lines.

Principle's inseparability from material force is really like the water's being inseparable from the vessel. Now if you would say that they mutually have issuances as function, then that would mean that sometimes the vessel would move first and the water would follow and move, sometimes the water would move first and the vessel would follow and move. How in the world could there be a rationale for this!

10.15b	And if one uses the metaphor of a man mounted on a horse, then the man is the nature, and the horse is the psychophysical constitution. The horse's temperament may be docile and good, or it may be indocile: this represents the differences of clarity and turbidity, purity and impurity in the psychophysical endowment. When they go out the gate, sometimes the horse follows the will of the rider and goes out; sometimes the rider leaves it to the horse and goes out. When the horse follows the will of the rider and goes out, it is classed on the side of the man: that is the Tao mind. When the man leaves it to the horse and goes out, it is classed on the side of the horse: that is the human mind. The road in front of the gate is the road of things and affairs as it ought to be traversed. When the rider has mounted the horse but not yet gone out the gate, there is no commencement or sign of either the man leaving it to the horse or the horse following the will of the man: this is the same as there originally being no systematic sprouts of the human mind and the Tao mind [in the not yet aroused mind-and-heart] that stand in contrast to each other.

> *In discussing travel as initiated by the rider or the rider leaving it to the horse, Yulgok sets up an explanation for different kinds of horse (docile and otherwise) as an easy parallel for the psychophysical constitution and its differences. However, the initiation by the rider versus initiation by the horse sounds a lot like T'oegye's double origin approach; as Ugye observes below (10.31a), such implicit dualism is hardly in keeping with Yulgok's metaphysics. Yulgok's analysis will eventually merge the initiation by the rider and the case of the docile horse following the proper way all by itself (10.27b), for there cannot be more than one way of explaining conduct in line with the norm.*

The vital forces of the sage are the same as those of other men: when they are hungry, they desire to eat; when thirsty, to drink; when cold, they want clothing; when they itch, they want to scratch. They likewise are not free from such matters. Therefore, the fact that even a sage must have a human mind is like the situation of having a horse that has a perfectly docile temperament; will there not be times when the rider goes forth, leaving it to the horse? But the horse is so submissive to the will of the rider that it does not wait for the reins to control it, but of itself follows the proper road: this is what is meant by the sage's "following the desires of his heart [without transgressing the norm],"[8] and the human mind being also the Tao mind.

In the case of ordinary persons, their psychophysical endowment is not perfectly pure, so when the issuance of the human

10.16a

mind is not controlled by the Tao mind, it devolves into evil. It is like the rider who goes forth, leaving it to the horse and not using the reins for control, so the horse has its way and does not traverse the proper road.

In this line of comparison, there is the case of a horse of the most indocile temperament. Even though the rider tries to control it with the reins, it bucks continually and inevitably runs off into wild groves and thickets of thorns. This is the case of a turbid and impure psychophysical endowment in which the human mind is in control, and the Tao mind is covered over and obscured. When the temperament of the horse is as indocile as this, the horse continually bucks without even a short period when it stands quietly: this is the condition of the man with a dark and confused mind-and-heart who has never established the Great Foundation.

Even if it is an indocile horse, if by chance it happens to stand still, then while it is standing still, there is no difference between it and the docile, good horse. This is like the situation of the ordinary man whose mind-and-heart is dark and confused, but even though he has not established its substance, there is by chance a period when his mind-and-heart is not yet aroused. At that moment, its clear and pure substance is no different from that of a sage.

From this kind of comparison, how can the explanation of the human mind and the Tao mind, and the matter of the predominance of principle or the predominance of material force be any-
10.16b thing but clear and easy to understand! If one wants to apply it to the mutual issuance thesis, it would be like the man and the horse being in different places when they have not yet gone out the gate, with the man mounting the horse after they go out. In some cases, the man might go out and the horse might follow him, in others the horse might go out and the man might follow. The terminology and the rationale both go wrong, and it becomes meaningless.

> *Ugye protests this caricature of T'oegye's position below (10.30b). Yulgok's view of the absolute consistency and insep-arability of the* li-ki *relationship is so strong that he sees the dualistic implications of any alternative with a clarity that leads him to portray the case in extreme terms.*

Nonetheless, a man and a horse can be separate from one another, so the comparison is not quite so close as that of the vessel and water. But water also has concrete form, and in this respect likewise is not comparable to principle, which is formless. Similes must be looked at flexibly; one cannot get mired in them.

In the psychophysical nature man receives at birth, there are certainly some cases in which good and evil are already determined. Therefore, Confucius said that "[at birth] persons' natures are close to being the same, but by the habituation of practice they become far different from one another."[9] And again he said, "The highest kind of wise man and the worst kind of fool do not change."[10] But that is not a matter of the original condition of [the fool's] nature, but the consequence of his darkness and confusion; hence, this cannot be called the equilibrium of the not-yet-aroused condition of the mind. The not-yet-aroused condition is the nature in its original condition. If there is darkness and confusion, then material force has already disrupted the nature. Therefore, this cannot be said to be the substance of the nature.

Having received your letter and carefully examined its intent, I feel that what you see is not wrong, but the way you express it is mistaken. The wording and tone of the letter I sent you were far too strong; I am embarrassed to think of it! What your letter says about being "too urgent in looking for agreement. How can one force it? It must wait upon meditative pondering and reflective examination,"[11]—that is perfectly correct. True principle calls for meditative pondering and a personal apprehension. If one just relies on the words of others, then one day he meets an eloquent speaker who holds that one thing is correct, and he is pleased with his words and accepts them, and the next he meets another eloquent speaker who maintains the opposite and is also pleased by his words and changes his opinion to follow him. When would one ever have a settled view?!

As for your proposition regarding splashing water at Willow Creek, it can be said to be seeing concrete things and thinking out the principle, but it seems still incomplete. For water's running downward is a matter of [natural] principle, but when splashed, it goes up into the hand, and this also is a matter of [natural] principle. If water only flowed downward and would not go upward even when splashed, that would be contrary to principle. When it splashes upward into the hand, although it is a matter of material force, that whereby it splashes upward into the hand is a matter of principle. Its splashing up into the hand is a matter of principle as mounted on material force. Seeking an original condition other than its mounting on material force is definitely wrong. If one takes cases where it is mounted on material force but [the issuance] is contrary to the constant [nature] and one calls it the original condition, that is also wrong. But if one sees that which is contrary to the constant [nature] and directly takes it as purely the product of material force alone and not something in which principle is present, that also is wrong. [As you mentioned,] for some [evil man] to grow old and die peacefully in his room is certainly contrary to what is normal. But when governance is unequal, and awards and punishments are not in accord with the proper norm, then there certainly is a rationale whereby evil men get their way and good ones suffer and perish. Mencius said, "That the small should serve the great and the weak serve the strong is natural."[12] Indeed, not taking into account the greatness or smallness of virtue but taking small or great only in terms of strength and weakness as that which determines victory or defeat, how could that be the original natural condition! It's just that he is speaking in terms of power, that's all. If power works that way, then the principle is also that way, and so he calls it "natural." That being the case, if a certain [evil] man manages to preserve his life, one may say that such is not the original nature of principle. But if one says that it is the sole product of material force and has nothing to do with principle, then it is wrong. Where in the world is there any material force apart from principle! (*This section most merits deep reflection. If one grasps this he can understand the wondrous inseparability of principle and material force.*)

10.17b

The wonder that is principle and material force is difficult to understand and difficult to explain. Principle has only a single wellspring, and material force likewise has only a single wellspring. Material force is evolvingly active and becomes diversified and uneven; principle likewise evolvingly acts and becomes diversified and uneven. Material force does not part from principle, and

10.18a

principle does not part from material force. This being the case, principle and material force are one. Where can one see any difference? As for what is described as "principle is just principle, material force is just material force,"[13] in what can one see that principle is just principle and material force just material force?

I hope that you will think this matter over carefully and then compose a response. I would like to find out what you come up with in your understanding of the matter.

CHAPTER 16

Ugye's Fifth Letter to Yulgok

0.23a   . . . There's no need to say much about the explanation of the Four and Seven that contrasts them in terms of principle and material force: I have already set it aside. Now there remain only the two expressions, human mind and Tao mind, that I do not yet understand clearly; I venture to bring this up again. If I can break

0.23b   through on this point, then the doubts and obfuscation of my bewitchment with the twofold branch thesis will melt away and your urgent intent to arrive at agreement will be fulfilled and the effects of your "unflagging patience in instructing others"[1] will be almost fully realized.

As for what your letter says about the rationale of the nature and feelings basically having no mutual issuance of principle and material force, but rather all cases of the nature issuing forth as feelings being only a matter of material force issuing and principle mounting it, I would venture to ask for more exact evidence that the rationale is truly like that, so that even if Heaven and Earth were founded anew and we expected a latter-day sage to appear, there could be no contradiction or deceit in it. I would like once again to enter into a consideration of how it is that in the end it is so. How is it that Master Chu said the one arises [from material force], while the other originates from [principle]; how is it that [Ch'en Fu-hsi] said that this consciousness has cases of issuing from principle and cases of issuing from material force [cf. above, 10.19b]? How is it that from of old, theories have all regarded humanity and rightness as pertaining to the issuance of principle and consciousness, movement, food and sex, and the psychophysical constitution as pertaining to material force?

Man's five viscera and one hundred bones all have this principle and are endowed with this physical form. Now with regard to
the norm for things, in the nature-feelings issuance, principle pre-
dominates, and it is permissible to speak of the subtle wellsprings
of good and evil. So what need is there to speak of the human
mind and Tao mind as issuing following principle or following
material force? Is it not that this material force is able to predomi-
10.24a   nate over the psychophysical constitution, and is able to be excessive and able to be deficient, being responsible for what it does
itself with principle not being able to govern and control it? In
your letter, although the human mind and Tao mind involve the
difference of whether principle or material force is the predominant factor, the origination is entirely a matter of principle and the
issuance is entirely a matter of material force. [According to you]
the expression, "the one arises . . . while the other originates" is
designed to refer to the condition after [the mind-and-heart] has
given issuance and to pick out its main characteristic. If one explains it like this, is it not simple and easy to understand?

Nevertheless, if this were really Master Chu's intent, he
should have changed the text to explain it like that, along the lines
of the ideas of his Diagram on Making the Incipient Wellsprings
[of the Mind-and-Heart] Sincere,[2] rather than saying "the one
arises . . . the other originates." As for the proposition that "the
one arises . . . while the other originates," with one following
from principle and the other from material force, I am stupid and
dull and do not know whether this view is the same as in your
letter or not. The expressions "arise from this," "originate from
this," "follow from principle," and "follow from material force,"
and so on, make it seem that principle and material force are two
distinct things that preexist here, and the human mind or the Tao
mind arises from the one or originates from the other, following a
certain one and issuing forth. You are good at explaining how the
various sorts of explanations of moral principle all have their
place. I wish you to make a detailed elaboration of how this original proposition [of Chu Hsi's] can fit with what you present in
10.24b   your letter.

I formerly had only roughly heard something of moral principle and roughly had some basis [for my understanding]. I had always regarded Master T'oegye's position as dubious, but when I saw [Master Chu's] interpretation of the human mind and Tao mind, my thinking became disordered, and my ideas all mixed up, and I was extremely upset. I wanted to decisively follow T'oegye's thesis, and yet could not quite swallow it and be at peace. But if I try to abandon it and hold onto my former views, this "the one arises . . . the other originates" proposition blocks my way and will not go away. My view of moral principle is not accurate, and so I am shaken and deluded. This vessel of our intimate relationship keeps on being unfilled with any attainment. I am unable to read books, unable to exercise subtle thought: this life is really pitiful!

CHAPTER 17

Yulgok's Reply to Ugye's Fifth Letter

10.21b How have you been recently? Have you looked carefully at the long letter I sent you yesterday? During the day, while I was sitting at leisure, I was moved at the wondrousness of principle and material force's being fundamentally without any separation or conjunction, and accordingly wrote a short verse about it and am sending it along. If we agree on this, there will be nothing on which we do not agree.

But you already understand that principle and material force cannot be separated for a blink of an eye, and yet you are still attached to the mutual issuance thesis; no matter how much I think about this, I cannot understand the reason. Is it not perhaps that you are bound up by the "the one originates . . . while the other arises" proposition and are unable to move? Master Chou [Tun-i] said, "The Supreme Ultimate moves and gives rise to yang, is still and gives rise to yin."[1] How could there be anything wrong with these two phrases? But if one misinterprets them, he will certainly take it to mean that originally there was no yin and yang, and the Supreme Ultimate existed before them. Then after the Supreme Ultimate moved, yang arose, and after the Supreme Ultimate was still, yin arose. To read it thus is a great misunderstanding of the original meaning, but as an interpretation it is quite in accord with the sentence structure and the words, and so would present no obstacle. It is the same in the case of the proposition regarding the one originating and the other arising.

Indeed, the Five Agents emerge from principle and material force, and their order is expressed in terms of "wood gives rise to

10.22a

fire, fire gives rise to earth." Now if one gets mired in the words and says that fire must necessarily arise from wood and is not based on principle, would that be permissible? That which issues the Tao mind is material force; but if it were not for the normative nature, the Tao mind would not be issued. That which originates the human mind is the nature, but if it were not for the psychophysical constitution, the human mind would not be issued. Is it not in accord with this to describe the Tao mind as originating with the normative nature and the human mind as arising from the psychophysical constitution? The psychophysical constitution giving rise to the human mind is likewise like the case of wood giving rise to fire. If you have already realized this, then this letter is superfluous, but if you have not, then it will be some help.

Verse on Principle and Material Force for Ugye, My Friend in Learning

Where is there a terminus of the original material force?
The formless is within that which has form;
Investigating the wellsprings one understands they are originally conjoined. (*Principle and material force are originally conjoined: they do not have a time when they began to be conjoined; one who would try to treat principle and material force as two would not have true understanding.*)
In the diverging flow of the streams one can see the varied subtleties; (*Principle and material force are originally one but are divided into the 'subtleties' of the two [forces, i.e., yin and yang] and the five [agents].*)
Water follows the square or round shaped bowl;
Space takes on the greatness or smallness of the vessel. (*That principle in mounting material force and becoming active is varied and not uniform is like this. The empty vessel explanation comes from the Buddhists, but the metaphor is appropriate so I have used it.*)
In the twofold branches let the gentleman not be entranced,
But in silence let him experience the nature as the feelings.

The nature is a composite of principle and material force, for

only after principle is within material force is it the nature. If it is
10.22b not within the psychophysical constitution, it should be called
principle; it should not be called the nature. But when one approaches the condition in which it is within the psychophysical
constitution but selectively speaks with reference only to principle,
then it is the "original nature." The original nature cannot have
material force mixed in. Tzu Ssu and Mencius referred to the original nature; Master Ch'eng and Master Chang [Tsai] referred to the
psychophysical nature. The actuality is the same, but the predominant factor they had in mind as they spoke of it was not. Now, if
one does not understand what was intended by what they regarded
as the predominant factor and just concludes that there are two
natures, could that be called understanding principle? Since the
nature is already single, if one considers the feelings differentiated
into the issuance of principle and the issuance of material force,
could that be called understanding nature?

My temperament is divorced from the contemporary world;
although I have had quite a bit of interaction with others, only you
fit well with me, and if you haven't rejected me, it must be because our sense of things is not different. If we and our views are
still not the same, then my solitude in my learning is too extreme!
Variant views in which there are differences and agreements are
an unavoidable part of being a scholar. But this is the great cornerstone of moral principle, the place where right and wrong, the
heretical and the true are differentiated; on this, it is not permissible to disagree. My having reiterated my views to such an extent
has not been just for your sake; I likewise have been regretting my
solitariness.

10.23a Nowadays, there are few among the so-called investigators of
principle with whom one could speak of these matters. Those who
would think it strange and declare it wrong are certainly not worth
mentioning. And as for those who would view it and declare themselves in agreement, one likewise could not trust that they really
understood. Song Unjang[2] and his brother are the only ones with
whom one could talk about this, and I am very much taken with
them; you likewise should not take them lightly. If An Sŭpji
comes, how about trying to talk to him? I rarely see the gentle-

man, but I suspect that he gives only general agreement and is not able to exercise the minute thought or deep inquiry that brings strong mutual confidence. I am not sure how he would react if he saw this.

CHAPTER 18

Ugye's Sixth Letter to Yulgok

> *In this letter, Ugye opposes Yulgok's dualistic view of*
> *T'oegye's position with his own most effective interpretation of*
> *the point of T'oegye's analysis. He accurately brings out appar-*
> *ently dualistic elements in Yulgok's own examples that are simi-*
> *lar to what Yulgok is opposing in T'oegye. This in turn will push*
> *Yulgok in his final letter to his fullest and most original expres-*
> *sion of what he considers the essence of the metaphysics of* li
> *and* ki.

10.30b   . . . How could what T'oegye speaks of as mutual issuance really be as your letter describes it, saying that it means that principle and material force are each in their own place mutually issuing as function? It's just that they are rolled up into a single thing, but there is the predominance of principle and the predominance of material force, that which emerges from within and that which is stimulated from without—beforehand, there are these two proclivities. What I meant when I said that, in the interchange of the nature and the feelings, there originally are principle and material force as two things each emerging on its own should also be looked at like this. How could it mean what you describe as the rider and horse each standing up and going out the gate following one another and catching up only afterward? My writing skill is insufficient, so my way of expressing it is too heavy-handed, and that is what I am guilty of.

     What you early and late earnestly try to convey just amounts to stating that in the interchange of the nature and feelings there is material force issuing and principle mounting it, this single mode and that is all; there is nothing else. As for my accepting this statement, how would I not wish to take it and use it as learning that is simple and easy to understand? But when I examine the question in terms of the former words of the sages and worthies, they all set up dualistic explanations and have nothing like your fine instruction. Therefore, I cannot venture to accept it.

10.31a   The last long letter you sent me said:

> When they go out the gate, sometimes the horse follows the will of the rider and goes out, sometimes the rider leaves it to the horse and goes out. When the horse follows the will of the rider and goes out, it is classed on the side of the man: that is the Tao mind. When the man leaves it to the horse and goes out, it is classed on the side of the horse: that is the human mind. [10.15b]

And again you say:

> The fact that even a sage must have the human mind is like the situation of having a horse that has a perfectly docile temperament; will there not be times when the rider goes forth, leaving it to the horse? [10.15b]

When I examine these sections, they all are dualistic explanations, and I suspect that they are somewhat different from the unitary statement that there is only material force issuing and principle mounting it; rather, they seem to gradually approach the ancient types of explanation.

Moreover, in reading your present letter I find that it says:

> That which issues the Tao mind is material force, but if it were not for the normative nature, then the Tao mind would not be issued. That which originates the human mind is the nature, but if it were not for the psychophysical constitution, the human mind would not be issued. Then is it not appropriate to regard the Tao mind as originating from the normative nature and the human mind as arising from the psychophysical constitution? [10.22a]

When I saw this paragraph, I agreed with its meaning and felt great admiration for the precision and aptness of the way it is expressed.

Nevertheless, in this as well there are some aspects that have not yet been thoroughly examined. You insist on saying that material force issues and principle mounts it, and there is no other mode. As for me, I insist on saying that although in the not-yet-aroused condition, there are no incipient shoots of principle and material force each having their own function, just as soon as it is aroused in the movement of intention and desire, there should be a predominance of principle or a predominance of material force that can be spoken of. It's not that each emerges [separately]; it's a matter of approaching the single mode and selecting its predominant character for reference.

0.31b

This is identical with what is meant by T'oegye's mutual issuance, which is the same as what you describe as the horse following the will of the rider or the rider leaving it to the horse [10.15b], that is, as you say, if it were not for the normative nature, the Tao mind would not be issued; if it were not for the psychophysical constitution, the human mind would not be issued. I wonder what you think of this? I pray most earnestly that you will exercise your utmost discernment on this point and analyze its ultimate implications minutely and let me know. On this matter, if we do not finally agree, then we finally do not agree.

Nonetheless, with regard to T'oegye's mutual issuance thesis, those who really know something will be concerned about its confused intricacy, and when the more ignorant read it, it is quite likely to mislead them. This is all the more so insofar as with respect to the Four and Seven, the positions of principle and material force are differentiated with two sorts of issuance distinguished as [material force] following [in one case] and [principle] mounting [in the other]; here the meaning of the words [used in the explanation] is not in close accord with the rationale of the terms [being explained]. Being uneasy about this is what has made me unhappy [with T'oegye's position].

10.32a

Your letter talks about being in accord and agreeing while bemoaning the loneliness of your position, but I do not think it necessarily has to be that way. As regards the Tao, the Superior

Man, if he has the actuality of profound attainment through personal apprehension, even should no one in the whole world be in accord with him his mind-and-heart will be at rest, his spirit harmonious, and he will take pleasure in the Tao with no regrets.[1] Po-i[2] was not concerned even on the day he starved to death, much less should you! When it comes to being concerned about the Tao not being transmitted or there being no one fit for studying the Tao, in that case one cannot but be concerned. It's only that when it comes to such an extremely large, extremely subtle and mysterious principle, one cannot expect a great awakening in a single morning, or to consume it all in a single mouthful. In this kind of learning, it is necessary to follow what you see to advance your view further, deepening it with actual practice, nurturing it for a long, long time, reflecting on it with a clearly focused mind-and-heart and silent recognition, with your mind-and-heart penetrating all about you and meeting it like [an outflowing] spring;[3] only then will one have apprehended it.

As for someone like me, who is sick and dull, a dying man with spent vitality, how could I be up to the subtle reflection and actual practice that brings the fruits of personal apprehension? But you have been endowed with a refinement that sets you apart from others, and others cannot rival it. But in such a case, deep confidence in oneself should come as when the fruit has thoroughly ripened and drops by itself. One cannot force this maturing and become puffed up with a certain vain arrogance that rushes out with high self-esteem. I'm not saying that you now have such a problem. But men of even the highest intelligence cannot neglect discerning whether there is anything of the sort in their persons.

10.32b

Your last letter contained quotations and questions aimed at putting my view to the test. Today I am worn out with trying to think deeply and my mind is exhausted, so I do not wish to try to think it through profoundly. Therefore, I am making no response to the items with which you find fault.

But while I was looking over your letter a thought suddenly came into my head: with respect to the dissimilarity between principle and material force, material force, from the moment it is involved with concrete form, has excesses and deficiencies. Their dissimilarity has to do with this and that is all. I don't know about this idea; I should elaborate on it more fully later. I also hope that you will match it with sending your thoughts and follow along with my ignorance.

When Sŭpji comes, I should show him all our earlier and later discussions, not only this one poem. However, Sŭpji's nature is distracted and distant from the pursuit of learning; the intent of seeking evidence in actual affairs, efforts at personally questioning and reflecting on things at hand, subtle thought and exact discrimination, personally experiencing [moral principle] and enlarging and fulfilling [its beginnings in our nature]—these are not his strong points. Thus, as for these letters, he will be able to read them over only once and that is all. I hope that you will rebuke him for this attitude and persuade him to abandon his former habits and reform.

And as for the issuance of the feelings having two kinds of proclivities, the predominance of principle and the predominance of material force, this clearly is the case, as is evinced in your
10.33a   example of the horse following the rider's will and the rider trusting where the horse goes. It's not that there are these proclivities before [the mind-and-heart] is aroused; but as soon as [the feelings] issue, there is [this differentiation] of originating from principle or arising from material force. It's not that principle gives issuance and material force follows afterward, or material force issues and then principle mounts it. For principle and material force have a single issuance and one approaches its predominant aspect and speaks in terms of the predominance of principle or the predominance of material force.

CHAPTER 19

Yulgok's Reply to Ugye's Sixth Letter

> *Ugye's letter made it clear that the appeal to metaphor or*
> *the reiteration of conventional expressions would not clarify*
> *what, for Yulgok, is the heart of the issue. Thus, in this letter,*
> *Yulgok is finally driven to present his thinking in its most per-*
> *sonal and original form: "I will now empty out all I have."*
> *What he has reserved until now is his own interpretation of the*
> *meaning of the distinction of* li *and* ki. *The conventional descrip-*
> *tion speaks of* li *as being "above" (or before) the world of ac-*
> *tual phenomena ("form") and hence non-active, while* ki *be-*
> *longs to that concrete level and so is active. His personal*
> *expression of the relationship is "i t'ong ki kuk," which I have*
> *rendered as "principle pervades and material force delimits."*
> *This letter is famous for his introduction and exposition of this*
> *interpretation. For generations to come, disciples in his school*
> *of thought would revere this expression as the crystalization of*
> *his central metaphysical insight.*

10.24b   How have you been since last night? I received your copious
and elegant letter yesterday. I was very happy to see a sign that we
may perhaps hope to reach an agreement. I have composed a long
letter discussing principle and material force and sent it to you
separately; please look it over in detail, and let me know what you
think of it.

What you said in your letter about material force being involved with what has form and concreteness, and in this respect
not the same as principle, is certainly a general statement of the
matter. But it involves several complex details that must be fully

10.25a investigated and completely thought out before we can say that we have grasped its full meaning. The explanation in my long letter is quite detailed; my original intention was to leave it at that, with the expectation that you yourself would take up the discussion. But now that I have received your inquiry to get to the bottom of it, if I do not fully explain it to the limit and examine the fundamental source of the issue, then to the very end, there can be no hope of our reaching an agreement. Therefore, I will now empty out all I have. This will all be what was meant by the sages and worthies, but it has been scattered throughout the classics and commentaries, and has not been synthesized; therefore, I am now combining it into this explanation, that is all.

"Principle pervades and material force delimits" (*i t'ong ki kuk*)—these four words I consider my own discovery, but I fear that my reading is not extensive, so these words may already be someplace and I have just not yet seen them. Taking the Tao mind as material force in its original condition likewise seems to be a new expression; although it is what is meant by the sages and worthies, I have not yet seen it in a text. If you do not question these expressions or think them too strange and reject them, then there is nothing upon which we will not agree.

By the way, I deeply appreciated your efforts yesterday to help with the transport of Sowa's lumber. Yesterday I received a letter from Kyeham; there is a message that my son is very anxious to quickly convey, so I sent an errand boy. In Kyeham's letter, he said my being slandered is of late becoming even more serious: there is even going to be a criminal proceeding. My person is already attached to the process of creation and transformation [in the universe]: shall a rat's liver or an insect's leg[1] try to take over **10.25b** responsibility for its course? But when I think carefully about what I have done, there is nothing that should cause others to hate or envy me. The only thing in my conduct any different from what is ordinary is my not serving in government, that is all. If they hate me like an enemy because I differ from them, then the way of the world can indeed be described as perilous. From of old, I have never heard of not serving in government as a crime, and if it now starts with me, then that likewise will be something to be laughed at in this age of decline. But now, when the nation is facing a great problem, if I do not work in office with others but rather journey afar, then there would be something questionable about the rightness of such conduct. Therefore, I have canceled my trip to the southeast and plan to send someone instead to my younger brother's place to have him go and present an offering at the tomb of Master T'oegye. How about your sending an offering as well? Yesterday I heard that Sa'am has been appointed a minister of the Right; the news [of developments] at court these days sounds like it really suits the needs of the situation, but I do not know whether it will prove effective or not in the end.

Letter on Principle and Material Force

Principle and material force are originally inseparable and seem to be a single thing; that in which they are different is that principle has no concrete form but material force does, principle is non-active, but material force is active. That which is formless and non-active and is the master of that which has form and is active is principle. That which has form and is active and is the instrument of that which is formless and non-active is material force. Principle is formless, and material force has form; therefore, principle pervades, and material force delimits. Principle is non-active, and material force is active; therefore, material force issues, and principle mounts it.

10.26a

> *This passage reflects the common Neo-Confucian understanding in which the "non-activity" and "formless" character of* li *are higher values compared to the concrete form and activity associated with* ki. *This makes* li *the "master," the norm for the way all activity should unfold. The following passage is a wonderful exposition of why these characteristics bear such an evaluation in a Neo-Confucian setting. This is important because the high value the modern world puts upon the concrete and material side of existence easily leads to interpretations that glorify Yulgok for exalting* ki, *which does not seem to be his intention.*

What does it mean to say that principle pervades? Principle has no origin or end, no before or after. Having no beginning or end, no before or after, therefore the condition of not yet having responded is not anterior, nor is the condition of having responded posterior (*the thesis of Master Ch'eng*).[2] Thus when it mounts material force and is involved in activity, there are innumerable differences and varieties, but the wondrousness of its original condition is nowhere absent. When material force is one-sided, then principle is likewise one-sided, but the one-sidedness owes not to principle, but to material force. When material force is integral (*chŏn*), principle is likewise integral, but the integrity owes not to principle, but to material force. When it comes to the clear or the turbid, the pure or the mixed, be it sediment, ashes, manure, or filth, principle is in the midst of all of them as the nature of each, and the wonder of its original condition does not hinder their being what they are. This is what is characterized as the pervasiveness of principle.

> T'ong *literally means to "pass through" or "penetrate." Being "above forms," li is not subject to the constraints of space and time; its fullness is pervasive and undiminished, regardless of the degree of limitation or distortion that might be introduced by the psychophysical component (ki). Yet it does not exist like a Platonic form in some realm apart; it is the actual norm making all concrete form and activity possible, and, as Yulgok emphasizes, exists in strict interdependence with ki. It is at once psychophysically embodied and still passes beyond (t'ong) the limits of concrete facticity. Thus, as actual fact, the happenstance of integral perfection is as much on the side of ki as is imperfection.*

What does it mean to say that material force delimits? Material force is already involved with concrete form; therefore, it has a beginning and end and anterior and posterior. In its original condition, material force has a translucent unity and clear emptiness and that is all. How could it ever be the material force of sediment, ashes, manure, or filth! It's only that it ascends and descends, and flies about without ever ceasing; therefore, there are innumerable differences and varieties, and the myriad changes arise. Since material force is in the active process, there are cases in which it does

10.26b

not lose its original condition, and other cases in which it does lose it. When it has lost its original condition, then the original condition of material force is not present in any way. The one-sided is one-sided material force, not integral material force. The clear is clear material force, not turbid material force. Sediment and ashes have the material force of sediment and ashes, not the translucently unified clear and empty material force. It's not like the presence of principle in the myriad things, wherein the wondrousness of its original condition is present in all. This is what is characterized as "material force delimits."

What does it mean to say that material force issues and principle mounts it? Yin being still and yang moving is from a natural mechanism; there is nothing or no one that makes them like that. When yang moves, then principle mounts the movement; it's not that principle moves. When yin is still, principle mounts the stillness; it's not that principle is still. Therefore, Master Chu says, "The Supreme Ultimate is the wondrousness of the original condition. Movement and rest are the mechanisms upon which it mounts."[3] Yin being still and yang moving are natural mechanisms, and that whereby yin is still and yang moves is principle. Therefore, Master Chou [Tun-i] says, "The Supreme Ultimate moves and gives rise to yang, is still and gives rise to yin."[4] Indeed, saying that it moves and gives rise to yang, and is still and gives rise to yin is predicated upon its not having been so [previously]; saying that movement and rest are the mechanisms upon which it mounts looks to the condition that is already so. Movement and stillness have no terminus; yin and yang have no beginning. So the proceeding to act of principle and material force belongs entirely to the condition of the already so, that is all. How could there be a time when it was not yet so? Therefore, the transformative process of Heaven and Earth and the issuance of our minds-and-hearts are all a matter of material force giving issuance and principle mounting it.

What is meant by saying that material force gives issue and principle mounts it is not that material force precedes principle. Material force has activity, and principle is non-active, so the expression cannot be otherwise. Indeed, in the province of principle, not one word can be added, not a single bit of effort toward the practice of self-cultivation applied. Principle is originally good: how can one apply cultivation to it? All the thousands and ten thousands of words of the sages and worthies are for the purpose of getting people to restrain and curb their material force so that they can restore their material force to its original condition, and that is all. The original condition of material force is when it is the "vast moving power" (Kor., *ho yŏn chi ki;* Chin., *hao-jan chih ch'i*).[5] When the "vast moving power" fills all between Heaven and Earth, then the original goodness of principle will not be hidden or obscured in the slightest. It is in this respect that Mencius's discussion of nurturing one's material force has been a contribution to the sagely tradition.

If material force issuing and principle mounting it were not the unique way, but rather principle as well could have a separate active function, then one could not say that principle is non-active. Why then did Confucius say: "It is man that can make the Tao great, not the Tao that makes man great"?[6] If we analyze it this way, then it is perfectly clear and settled that material force issuing

10.27b   and principle mounting it is the sole way. And the other questions—the one originating while the other arises [statement of Chu Hsi], the rider trusting where the horse will go and the horse being obedient to the will of the rider—these we will also be able to comprehend thoroughly and grasp in their ultimate significance. Please try to reflect on this carefully and think it out in detail; do not just treat what I say lightly because of my shallowness and superficiality.

The proposition that material force issuing and principle mounting it is the sole way, and the propositions regarding the one originating and the other arising, the rider trusting where the horse goes and the horse being obedient to the will of the rider—these can all be comprehended [in the same way]. You have not yet gotten to that point, and therefore you have not been able to completely rid yourself of T'oegye's theses that principle and material force mutually give issuance, that [one kind of feeling] emerges from within, while another is externally stimulated, and that there are beforehand two sorts of proclivities; rather, you try to take

T'oegye's propositions and attach them to mine. I have [already] separately presented a quite detailed discussion of this, but I fear that you have not yet thoroughly gotten the point. For the thesis that material force issuing and principle mounting it is the sole mode is a proposition that gets to the foundation of the matter. The one originating and the other arising, or the rider trusting where the horse goes and the horse obeying the master, are derivative propositions.

> *This is Yulgok's definitive response to the dualistic implications that can be found in authoritative sources and, as Ugye has indicated, even in his own imagery. The mutual difference and interdependence of* li *and* ki *as expressed in his "*li *pervades and* ki *delimits" formula provides the framework within which various sayings and images must be interpreted. The events of the concrete world of space and time all happen in terms of* li, *but* ki *contrasts with* li *precisely as the concretizing, energizing component that accounts for all facticity.*

Now when you say that with regard to the condition before [the mind-and-heart] is aroused, there are no systematic sprouts of principle and material force each having a function, it is in agreement with my view. But when you say that in the interchange of the nature and the feelings there is originally principle and material force as two [distinct] things each emerging on its own, this is not only a mistake in the way of expressing it, it is in fact a mistaken point of view. And then again you say [the Four and the Seven] is a matter of approaching one side and taking its predominant aspect to refer to it—this again is in agreement with my view. In the course of the one letter, at one moment we agree and at another disagree. Although there is some inaccuracy in what you see, this indicates that you are just at the point of believing and at the point of doubting, and that means that you are at the point of having the subtle beginning of a breakthrough. Now if you understand that the proposition regarding material force issuing and principle mounting it flows together with the rider trusting where the horse goes and the horse obeying the rider's will as a single thesis, then

0.28a

there will be no room for any further doubt that we will reach an agreement.

The Tao mind originates from the normative nature, but that which gives it issuance is material force, so it is wrong to describe it as principle giving issuance. The human mind and the Tao mind are both alike the issuance of material force. But material force in some cases is submissive to principle in its original condition, so the material force is also then in the original condition of material force. Therefore, when principle mounts this material force that is in its original condition, it is the Tao mind. Material force in some cases changes principle from its original condition, so it is itself changed from the original condition of material force. Therefore, principle likewise mounts on the changed material force and is the human mind, which is at times excessive and at times deficient. Sometimes at the beginning, when it has just issued forth, the Tao mind is already in control, and it does not allow it to become excessive or deficient. At other times, after there has been excess **10.28b**   or deficiency, the Tao mind likewise takes control and makes it quickly return to equilibrium.

> *If there is a weakness in Yulgok's position, it is that everything seems to depend ultimately on material force. This is evident in the first and more analytic half of this paragraph. But such an interpretation of Yulgok is itself a matter of an overly dualistic analysis that forgets that nothing on the level of actual existence can be understood in terms of either* li *or* ki *alone. Yulgok, with his emphasis on interdependence, has no problem returning in the latter part of the paragraph to language that suggests an activist role coming from the normative (Tao mind) side. After his analysis, he is confident that such normative tendencies can be understood in terms of the unitary whole in which the normative force of* li *is rendered concrete and effective through* ki. *Only when analysis separates them and forgets that they originally and always belong together does one run into the problem of regarding the non-active, transcendent status of* li *as meaning it is an empty cypher when it comes to concrete activity. When he is speaking in his analytic mode, however, Yulgok's language can easily give the impression that everything ultimately hangs on* ki. *The following paragraph, especially in its final sentence, is a good example of the problem.*

When material force is submissive to principle in its original condition, it is definitely a case of material force issuing, but the material force obeys the governance of principle. Therefore, what is predominant lies with principle, and it is referred to in terms of the predominance of principle. Material force's being changed in accord with the original condition of principle definitely is a matter of [the condition] originating from principle and that is all. But if it is not material force in its original condition, it cannot be said to be obeying the governance of principle. Therefore, the predominant factor lies with material force, and it is referred to in terms of the predominance of material force. Whether or not material force obeys the governance is entirely a matter of how material force acts; as for principle, it is non-active: one cannot say that they mutually have an issuance function.

It is only in the case of a sage that the psychophysical constitution always obeys the governance of principle so that the human mind is likewise the Tao mind. So one should differentiate them in one's discussion; one may not run them together as a single proposition. Moreover, Master Chu said, "The emptiness, spirituality, and consciousness of the mind-and-heart are one, and that is all."[7] As for his proposition that "the one originates from the correctness of the normative nature, while the other arises from the self-centered proclivities of the psychophysical constitution,"[8] one should preface it with the word "mind-and-heart" [as Chu Hsi did]. But the mind-and-heart is a matter of material force. The one originating and the other arising is nothing but the issuance of the mind-and-heart, so how can they not be the issuance of material force? The principle possessed within the mind-and-heart is the nature. There is no rationale whereby the mind-and-heart gives issuance but the nature does not; so is that not principle mounting on [material force]? "The one originates . . ." is so said in view of cases in which principle is the predominant thing; "the other arises . . ." is so said in view of cases in which material force is the predominant thing. It's not that at the beginning there are principle and material force as two systematic sprouts. In establishing teachings to enlighten people, there was no alternative to speaking like this, and whether or not scholars might have mistaken views of it was not for Master Chu to anticipate.

0.29a

Seen in this way, are the propositions that material force issues and principle mounts it and that the one originates while the other arises in the end much opposed to each other? If you make your judgment of this and do not agree, then I fear that it will end with our not being able to agree. As for T'oegye's two words "mutual issuance," it seems that they were not just a mistake in expressing himself: I'm afraid it was a matter of his not being able to see deeply enough into the mystery of the inseparability of principle and material force.

Moreover, there is his differentiation of [some feelings] emerging from within and [others] being stimulated externally, which is very different from my view. And your wishing to take his and assimilate it to mine is not only a matter of not understanding in what my meaning consists, it is also a matter of not being able to clearly understand what T'oegye meant. For T'oegye regarded what emerges from within as the Tao mind and what is externally stimulated as the human mind. For my part, I regard both the human mind and Tao mind as emerging from within and the movement in both cases as being stimulated externally. Do these in the end agree, and can you take them and bring them together? You should take T'oegye's original text and my earlier

10.29b and later letters and look them over again and try to see what they are getting at.

In the nature and the feelings, there is fundamentally no rationale for the mutual issuance of principle and material force. That all cases of the nature issuing forth as feelings are only a matter of material force issuing and principle mounting it, and so on, is not just something I made up; it is what was meant by former Confucians. It's just that they had not yet spoken in detail on the matter, and I only extrapolated their meaning, that is all. If Heaven and Earth were to be fashioned anew, there would be no contradicting this; even if one awaited the coming of a later sage, there could be no deceit in it. It is certain beyond doubt.

Wherein do I find what was meant by former Confucians? Did not Master Chu say, "The psychophysical nature is just this nature (*"this nature" means the original nature*)[9] as it has descended into the midst of the psychophysical constitution; therefore, it follows the psychophysical and of itself is as our single nature" (*"nature" here meaning the psychophysical nature*).[10] Master Ch'eng has said: "The nature is identical with material force, material force is identical with the nature; this is what is meant by 'that which is so at birth [is the nature].'"[11]

Considered in these terms, the psychophysical nature and the original nature are certainly not two natures. It's just that when one approaches the psychophysical constitution and only points out its principle, it is called the original nature, and when one combines principle and material force [in one's reference], it is termed the psychophysical nature. Since the nature is but one, how can feelings have two origins? Only if there are two natures can there be two sorts of feelings. In the case of T'oegye's thesis, it is as if the original nature is in the east and the psychophysical nature in the west: what emerges from the east is called the Tao mind and what emerges from the west is called the human mind. How is that reasonable?! If one says that there is one nature, and then again goes on to say that what emerges from the nature is the Tao mind and that which emerges of itself without the nature is the human mind, is that reasonable either? "When words are not in accord [with the reality of things] then affairs cannot be successfully carried out."[12] I hope you will give this thorough consideration.

The words I used in the explanation of the diagram the other day were not meant to expound what former sages had not discovered. As for the diagram's expressions, "originating from humanity and on the contrary doing violence to humanity," and so on, although they express what was meant by former worthies, none of them said it clearly. Those of superficial views will certainly suspect it of contradicting the explanations of former worthies, and so I have mentioned it. How about "not letting the words get in the way of the meaning"?[13]

Notes

Introduction

1. The Ch'eng-Chu school of thought formed the central or "orthodox" tradition of Chinese Neo-Confucianism, its position established by its official status in the all important examinations for government service. Chu Hsi is the unequaled final authority in this school, but as will be described below, his synthesis adopted the thought of the Ch'eng brothers as its core, hence their names are joined with his.

2. Ch'eng Hao (honorific name Ming-tao, 1032–1085) and Ch'eng I (honorific name, I-chuan, 1033–1107).

3. Chou Tun-i's *Diagram of the Supreme Ultimate* actually came from a Taoist background, and the *Doctrine of the Mean*, which grounded Neo-Confucian meditative practice, was studied and valued by Buddhists long before Neo-Confucians gave it high prominence in the Confucian canon. The most prominent development of the concept of *li* was also under Buddhist auspices, notably in the Hwa Yen school. None of this was simply "borrowed" in crudely syncretistic fashion, but questions and expectations functioning in the elaboration of Neo-Confucian thought were deeply influenced by centuries during which the Taoist and Buddhist traditions had been at the center of intellectual and spiritual endeavor.

4. See *Book of Rites*, chap. 9.

5. *Mencius*, 2A6.

6. For the original and emended diagrams, together with T'oegye's long preface, cf. *TGCS*, A, 41.1a–11a.

7. This date is based upon the first reference to Kobong's (undated) postscript, which occurred in a letter of T'oegye's. The letter itself is undated, but immediately follows another to Kobong dated 1566 in his *Collected Works*.

8. The character *ssu* in many contexts means "selfishness," or "self-centeredness." Here it describes the personal separateness that goes with physicality. Insofar as the separateness of a person's physical needs are the occasion for self-centered distortion in our actions, the negative connotation is present even in this context.

Chapter 1

1. That is, T'oegye's amended version of Chŏng Chiun's *Diagram of the Heavenly Mandate*.

Chapter 2

1. *Mencius*, 2A6.

2. Cf. *YL*, 4.10b.

3. For the classical locus of the Seven Feelings cf. *Book of Rites*, chap. 9.

4. These are the expressions T'oegye used in his first letter, A1b.

5. The classical passage on the human mind and the Tao mind is *Book of Documents*, pt. 2, 2.15: "The human mind is perilous, the mind of the Tao is subtle; be discerning, be undivided. Hold fast the Mean!" This passage was the major classical sanction for the Neo-Confucian distinction between the perfectly good "original nature" and the "physical nature," i.e., the nature as subject to the imperfections of material force. The human mind and Tao mind become prominent concepts in the Yulgok-Ugye stage of the debate.

6. *Chung-yung chang-chü* (Chu Hsi's Commentary on *Doctrine of the Mean*), chap. 1.

Chapter 3

1. References to *Doctrine of the Mean*, chap. 1, and *Mencius*, 6A6, respectively.

2. *Mencius*, 6A6, refers to them as "hsin" (Kor. *sim*), a general term for inner dispositions in his period but meaning the "mind-and-heart" to Neo-Confucians.

3. T'oegye uses the *so chu* with causal overtones to designate *li* or *ki* as the main element in the arising of given feelings. For Kobong, the phrase indicates only the mental focus of the speaker. For further discussion of this important ambiguity, cf. below, comment to A12b.

4. *Chung-yung huo-wen*, 23a.

5. *Mencius*, 2A6.

6. *Mencius*, 6A6.

7. Reference to *Book of Changes*, Great Appendix A, 4.

8. *Analects*, 17.2 and *Mencius*, 7B24, respectively.

9. *I-ch'uan wen-chi*, 4.1a–2a.

10. Cheng-an was the honorific name of Lo Ch'in-shun (1465–1547), a leading Chinese Neo-Confucian thinker who was critical of the dualistic interpretation of principle and material force.

11. *YL*, 53.17b.

Chapter 4

1. *YL*, 5.11a–b.

2. *YL*, 5.2a.

3. *YL*, 5.7b.

4. *YL*, 5.10a.

5. *YL*, 5.9a.

6. *YL*, 53.17b. This is the Chu Hsi passage that gave T'oegye confidence in his thesis.

7. *YL*, 4.10a.

8. The above paragraph is Kobong's paraphrase of T'oegye's ideas as expressed in Section Six, A4a–4b.

9. As T'oegye notes below, A42a, this description of the diagram is inaccurate.

10. This is a polite section in which Kobong expresses his joy and surprise that T'oegye will condescend to discuss the matter with him.

11. *CTTC*, 58.21a–b. There are many similar passages in the *YL*; the development of the material force (physical nature) explication of evil necessitated repeated explanations of why Mencius's doctrine of human nature makes no mention of it.

12. Cf. A1b.

13. Cf. A1b.

14. *YL*, 10a–b.

15. *YL*, 4.10b.

16. *YL*, 4.11b.

17. *YL*, 4.10b.

18. *YL*, 4.12b.

19. I have been unable to locate the source of this passage.

20. The *Chung-yung chang-chü*. This is the standard interlinear commentary printed with most editions of the *Doctrine of the Mean*.

21. *Chung-yung huo-wen*, 16a–b.

22. It is possible that this title is an abbreviated reference to the *Ssu-shu chang-chü chi-chü*, the standard collection of the *Four Books* with Chu Hsi's interlinear commentaries.

23. Yen-p'ing is the honorific name of Chu Hsi's teacher, Li T'ung (1093–1163).

24. I have not been able to find the source of this passage.

25. *CTTC*, 67.8a–b.

26. *I-ch'uan wen-chi*, 4.1a.

27. *Book of Rites*, 37.

28. *CTTC*, 67.8a.

29. *CTTC*, 67.1a. Origination and so on are four qualities of the universe, as described in the *Book of Changes*. They were correlated both with the characteristics of the four seasons (the production and so forth mentioned here), and the four characteristics of human nature, humanity, righteousness, propriety, and wisdom. Such correlations manifest the one Tao/the unity of principle that runs through all existence.

30. Ibid.

31. I have not been able to find the source of this passage.

32. *Mencius*, 6B13.

33. *Analects*, 11.10, referring to Confucius's grief on the death of his favorite disciple, Yen Hui.

34. *Analects*, 11.13.

35. *I-shu*, 22.11a.

36. *Ta hsüeh huo wen*, 42b.

37. *Analects*, 17.2.

38. *Mencius*, 7B24.

39. *Meng-tzu chi-chu*, 7B24.

40. *YL*, 61.5b.

41. I cannot find this exact passage, but the identical thought and similar wording can be found in *YL*, 61.4a.

42. *Erh Ch'eng ch'üan-shu*, 18.15a.

43. *Lun yü chi-chu*, 9.16.

44. *YL*, 1.2b.

45. *Mencius*, 4B12: "The great man does not loose the mind of an innocent baby."

46. *CTTC*, 64.29a–b.

47. *[Yen Hui's] Love of Learning, I-ch'uan wen-chi*, 4.1a.

48. *Book of Rites*, 37.

49. *CTTC*, 42.5a.

50. *CTTC*, 46.27b–28a.

51. Ibid.

52. Yün-feng was the honorific name of Hu Ping-men, a noted scholar of the Yüan dynasty.

53. Chu Hsi's note in the *Ta-hsüeh chang-chü* says, "The intention is that which the mind-and-heart issues."

54. *Mencius*, 6A6.

55. This is the very same phrase T'oegye used.

56. The diagram appears in the *Hsing-li ta-ch'üan*, 29.5a–b.

57. The main issue Kobong takes up is the question of T'oegye's distinguishing the attributes of "emptiness" and "spirituality" (subtlety) in the mind-and-heart in terms of principle and material force respectively. This topic is peripheral to the main issues of the Four-Seven Debate

Chapter 5

1. Sectional divisions were not indicated in T'oegye's revised draft, but I have retained them to facilitate reference.

2. References to *Doctrine of the Mean*, chap. 1, and *Mencius*, 6A6, respectively.

3. *Mencius*, 6A6.

4. *Mencius*, 2A6.

5. Reference to *Book of Changes*, Great Appendix A, 4.

6. *Analects*, 17.2, and *Mencius*, 7B24, respectively.

7. *I-ch'uan wen-chi*, 4.1a–2a.

8. Cf. A3b.

9. *YL*, 53.17b.

10. I can find only twelve items.

11. Actually, Kobong addressed these remarks to the fourth section of T'oegye's letter.

12. Numbers are being added to the items T'oegye takes up for discussion, for Kobong refers to them by these numbers in his reply.

13. Chu Hsi used such language in describing Mencius's approach (cf. *YL*, 4.10b.).

14. The genesis of this imagery is particularly clear in a *YL* passage that responds to a question about Chu Hsi's "mounting" phrase in his commentary on the *Explanation of the Diagram of the Supreme Ultimate*: "Question: About movement and rest as the mechanism mounted [by the Supreme Ultimate]. Answer: The Supreme Ultimate is principle. Movement and rest are material force. When material force is active, principle likewise is active; the two are always interdependent and are never separated. The Supreme Ultimate is like a man and movement and the rest are like a horse: the horse is what carries the man, and the man is what mounts the horse. When the horse goes or comes the man also goes or comes" (*YL*, 94.10a).

15. Chŏng Chi-un's original version and T'oegye's amended version of the Diagram of the Heavenly Mandate may be found in *TGCS* A, 41.40b–41a. There are two circles, one representing the nature in itself, and the other the active/concrete nature. The former contains humanity, righteousness, propriety, and wisdom, the latter the corresponding Four Beginnings and the Seven Feelings.

16. Cf. above, A17a.

17. *YL*, 53.17b.

18. His amendment was to drop the second sentence ("Only after they have issued . . ."), while modifying the first sentence to convey that as soon as there is not discernment the mind-and-heart loses its proper condition. The overall change seems to be from the original idea that they are good only after proper control to the idea they are good so long as there is proper control, a nuance that grants more in the direction of recognizing their originally good rather than indeterminate condition. T'oegye likewise dropped the phrase that said they are indeterminate.

19. *Ming-tao wen-chi*, 3.1b. For a full translation of the letter, which is actually a reply by Ch'eng Hao to a letter of Chang Tsai regarding calming one's nature, see Chan, *A Sourcebook in Chinese Philosophy*, pp. 525–26.

20. *Analects*, 8.5.

21. In this section, T'oegye cites the case of Chou Tun-i's famous and controversial *Diagram of the Supreme Ultimate* as evidence against Kobong's argument that diagrams should avoid any elements that might mislead the ignorant. He then delivers another lecture on the flexible and contextualized approach one must use in reading the writings of the sages and worthies, taking care not to force passages to fit one's preconceived theories or absolutize one kind of expression at the expense of others. He then vigorously denies that his ideas of differentiating the Four Beginnings and Seven Feelings in terms of their point of origin in principle or material force have any connection with the kind of ideas circulating among contemporary conventional scholars or with the ideas of Hu Yün-feng, as implied by Kobong [cf. A24a–b].

22. A reference to a story in which two travelers read an inscription that one understood immediately, while the other understood it only thirty miles down the road.

Chapter 6

1. The English here picks up the ambiguity of the original. Kobong's expression "never meant two things" (*pi yu i* ["two"] *üi*) could mean either that there is no difference of meaning or that there is no existential difference in what is referred to—i.e., not two separate sets of feelings. T'oegye seems to be taking him in the former sense with his paraphrase, "mean something different" (*pi yu i* [the character for "different"] *üi*), or "have no different referent" (*mu i chi*). Kobong's objection here seems to indicate that the latter sense was his intent, and this is indeed in line with his general argument that the Seven Feelings include the Four Beginnings.

2. This is Kobong's response to T'oegye's listing and categorization of points of agreement and disagreement. It does not contain any substantive discussion of issues.

3. Kobong in this letter refers to the numerical order of the sections of T'oegye's response. The numbering used here by Kobong has been inserted in brackets into the text of T'oegye's letter for ease of reference.

4. *Hsing-li ta-ch'üan*, 30.3a. The passage as quoted in the *Hsing-li ta-ch'üan* ends here, but it is possible the next sentence also is part of it—as in fact Kobong's wording would lead one to expect. I have not been able to find it in Chu Hsi's original works to check.

5. The five constants are humanity, righteousness, propriety, wisdom, and sincerity, which are taken to be the constituent characteristics of human nature. The first four of these come from Mencius's discussion of the Four Beginnings, while sincerity was added in order to fill out the system of correspondences with a cosmology based on the five agents.

6. The yang animating principle associated with the psyche and the yin animating principle associated with the body.

7. *YL*, 53.17b.

8. Years later, T'oegye actually did this in chap. 6 of his *Ten Diagrams on Sage Learning*, cf. *TGCS*, A, 7.22b.

9. From Chu Hsi's *Diagram of the Nature*, cited by Kobong above, A25a.

10. *YL*, 1.2b.

11. The phrase "*il yu chi*" is ambiguous. T'oegye seems to take it to mean "as soon as you have them," in line with his emphasis on the need for discernment in the case of such feelings; that is the translation I have used thus far. But Kobong seems to take the "*il*" ("one" or "once") not in the "as soon as" sense, but simply as one, and thus I have translated the same passage here as "If you have but one." This is in line with his contention that there is no inherent unreliability in the Seven Feelings such as would really distinguish them from the Four Beginnings.

12. *YL*, 16.26a.

13. *YL*, 16.25b.

14. *Chung-yung huo-wen*, 19b. The text I have reads "certainly have" (*yu*) where Kobong quotes "certainly have no" (*wu*), which seems to be the more logical meaning of the passage.

15. *YL*, 53.7b.

16. Cf. comment, B11a.

17. *YL*, 1.2b–3a.

Chapter 7

1. *YL*, 53.17b.

2. *Doctrine of the Mean*, chap. 1.

3. Kobong's interlinear annotation.

4. *YL*, 4.10a.

Chapter 8

1. *CTTC*, 67.8a.

2. The passage in the *Book of Rites* being discussed by Chu Hsi is the *locus classicus* for the Seven Feelings.

3. *YL*, 53.17b.

4. Ibid. This is the last half of the passage T'oegye made the basis of his Four-Seven distinction, i.e., the passage in which Chu Hsi discriminates the Four Beginnings as the issuance of principle and the Seven Feelings as the issuance of material force (cf. above, A6b).

5. Kobong seems to understand this phrase as indicating that Chu Hsi is making a concession, i.e., although they are different, they certainly have some similarities.

6. Cf. B27a or *TGCS*, A, 17.23a. The letter is undated, but is preceded by another letter to Kobong dated 1566.

Chapter 9

1. *TGCS*, A, 7.24a–b.

2. That is, the human mind and the Tao mind. Cf. above, Chap. 2 n. 5.

3. Cf. *TGCS*, A, 7.22b.

Chapter 10

1. I have not been able to locate this passage.

Chapter 11

1. There is no letter from Ugye matching with this reply from Yulgok in the extant correspondence between the two. But both Ugye and

Yulgok in subsequent letters make passing references to this letter and to statements made by Ugye in the missing letter, so its position at this point in their correspondence is secure.

2. *I-shu*, 1.7b.

3. *I-ch'uan wen-chi*, 5.12b. This important saying originated in the context of a letter of Ch'eng I in defense of Chang Tsai's *Western Inscription*. For an English translation, see Chan, *Source Book*, pp. 550–51.

4. We do not have this letter.

Chapter 12

1. The character *ssu* in many contexts means "selfishness" or "self-centeredness." Here it describes the personal separateness that goes with physicality. Insofar as the separateness of a person's physical needs are the occasion for self-centered distortion in our actions, the negative connotation is present even in this context.

2. Cf. above, 10.9b.

Chapter 13

1. *Explanation of the Diagram of the Supreme Ultimate, Hsing-li ta-ch'üan*, 1.31a–b.

2. Ibid.

3. Reference to *Doctrine of the Mean*, chap. 1.

4. *Mencius*, 7A, 38.

5. A reference to Chang Tsai's *Western Inscription, Hsing-li ta-ch'üan*, 4.2b. For an English translation, see Chan, *Source Book*, p. 497.

6. *Record of Music, Book of Rites*, 19. This passage also figured prominently in the T'oegye-Kobong debate (cf. A16).

7. Cf. above, chap. 2 n. 5.

8. *Chung-yung chang-chü hsü* (Preface to Chu Hsi's Commentary on the *Doctrine of the Mean*). The full sentence reads: "The emptiness, spiri-

tuality and consciousness of the mind-and-heart are one and that is all, but it involves the differences of the Tao mind and the human mind."

9. *Book of Changes*, Appended Remarks, pt. 1, chap. 10.

10. Yulgok's annotation.

11. This is the same character translated as "beginnings" in the case of Mencius's Four Beginnings.

12. *Doctrine of the Mean*, chap. 1.

13. *I-shu*, 1.3b.

14. *CTTC*, 46.24a, Letter to Liu Shu-men.

15. Cf. T'oegye's similar but less admiring reference to Lo, above, A6a.

16. For an English translation, see Chan, *Source Book*, pp. 525–26.

17. *Mencius*, 6A3.

Chapter 14

1. See Chu Hsi's preface to the *Doctrine of the Mean*.

2. See, for example, *YL* 94.10a.

3. *Chung-yung chang-chü*, introductory remarks.

4. *Hsing-li ta-ch'üan*, 32.24b. Pei-hsi was the honorific name of Ch'en Ch'un (1153–1217), one of Chu Hsi's pupils.

5. This paragraph takes up matter discussed in Ugye's missing second letter and in Yulgok's response to it.

Chapter 15

1. *I-shu*, 1.7b.

2. *Book of Rites*, T'an kung A, in *Shih-san ching chu-shu*, p. 1290.

3. Yu Tzu and Tseng Tzu were both Confucius's disciples. When Yu Tzu heard this saying from Tseng Tzu, he flatly declared that such

could not be what Confucius meant. On further inquiry, it turned out that the two parts of the saying were uttered as expressions of indignation regarding an avaricious office holder and a son lacking in proper mourning, respectively; they were in no way meant as normative statements. See *Book of Rites*, ibid.

4. Sojae was the honorific name of No Susin (1515–1590); his courtesy name was Kwahoe. He questioned T'oegye's views on the Four-Seven issue and on the human mind and Tao mind. He eventually followed Wang Yang-ming and was reputed to be inclined toward Buddhist views.

5. *Analects*, 2:2.

6. The expression is borrowed from *Mencius*, 5A6, where the imperfect sons of the sages Yao and Shun are spoken of as "not resembling" their fathers.

7. In a very similar usage of the muddy water metaphor, Chu Hsi likewise concludes: "One may not regard the turbidity as not water; in the case of evil likewise, one cannot but call it the nature." *CTTC*, 67.17b.

8. *Analects*, 2:2.

9. *Analects*, 17:2.

10. Ibid.

11. Cf. above, 10.20a.

12. *Mencius*, 4A7.

13. I cannot find these exact words, but in a letter to Liu Shu-men, Chu Hsi comes close to this when he says, "Although it is located in the midst of material force, material force is just material force, and the nature is just the nature" (*CTCS*, 46.24b).

Chapter 16

1. *Analects*, 7:34, a phrase Confucius used to describe himself.

2. The diagram, in which Chu Hsi is clarifying Chou Tun-i's view of sincerity, is to be found in *Hsing-li ta-ch'üan*, 2.13a. It seems to imply a single origin of good and evil, with good being a straight line issuance

and evil an angled (distorted) issuance, similar to the way Yulgok handled the question in his diagram above, 9.38b.

Chapter 17

1. *Explanation of the Diagram of the Supreme Ultimate*, in *Hsing-li ta-ch'üan*, 1.5a.

2. Unjang was the courtesy name of Song Ikp'il (1534–1599), a scholar especially renowned for his literary abilities and ritual studies.

Chapter 18

1. Cf. *Mencius*, 4B14.

2. The son of a local ruler in twelfth-century China; he was famous for starving to death rather than change his allegiance to King Wen.

3. Cf. *Mencius*, 4B14.

Chapter 19

1. See *Chuang tzu*, chap. 6, where a dying man indicates his acceptance of a process that will transform him into a rat's liver or an insect's leg.

2. Yulgok's annotation. Cf. *I-shu*, 15.8a.

3. Chu Hsi's commentary on Chou Tun-i's *Explanation of the Diagram of the Supreme Ultimate*, *Hsing-li ta-ch'üan*, 1.5b.

4. *Explanation of the Diagram of the Supreme Ultimate*, ibid.

5. *Mencius*, 2A2.

6. *Analects*, 15.28.

7. Preface to the *Chung-yung chang-chü*. This statement immediately precedes the sentence about "originating" and "arising."

8. Ibid.

9. Yulgok's annotation.

10. *CTTC*, 58.14a.

11. *I-shu*, 1.7b.

12. *Analects*, 13.3.

13. Paraphrase of *Mencius*, 5A4.

Glossary

An Sŭpji　安習之
Chang Shih, Nan-hsien
　張栻, 南軒
Chang Tsai, Heng-ch'ü
　張載 橫渠
Ch'en Ch'i-chih　陳器之
Ch'en Ch'un, Pei-hsi
　陳淳, 北溪
Ch'en Fu-hsi *see* Ch'en Ch'un
Ch'eng Hao, Ming-tao
　程顥, 明道
Ch'eng Yi, I-ch'uan
　程頤, 伊川
Ch'eng Chu　程朱
Ch'ŏnmyŏng tosŏl　天命圖說
chŏn　全
Chŏng Chiun　鄭之雲
Chosŏn (dynasty)　朝鮮
Chou Tun-i　周敦頤
chu　主
Chu Hsi, Hui-an　朱熹, 晦菴
chu i　主理
chu ki　主氣
Chu Tzu ta-ch'üan　朱子大全
Chu Tzu yü-lei　朱子語類
Chung-yung chang-chü
　中庸章句

Chung-yung huo-wen
　中庸或問
Erh Ch'eng ch'üan-shu
　二程全書
Hanguk yuhak charyo
　chipsŏng　韓國儒學資料集成
Heng-ch'ü *see* Chang Tsai
hoyŏn, hao-jan　浩然
Hsi-shan *see* Ts'ai Yuan-ting
Hsing-li ta-chüan　性理大全
Hu Kuang-chung　胡廣仲
Hu Ping-men, Yün-feng
　胡炳文, 雲峰
Hua-yen　華嚴
Huang Kan, Mien-tsai
　黃幹, 勉齋
Hui-an, cf. Chu Hsi
Huo-wen *see* Chung-yung
　huo-wen and Ta-hsüeh
　huo-wen
Hwadam *see* Sŏ Kyŏngdŏk
hyŏlmaek　血脈
hyŏngjil　形質
i, li *see* li
I-shu　遺書
il　一
il yu chi　一有之

201

insŏl 因說
ki, ch'i 氣
Ki Taesŭng, Myŏngŏn, Kobong 奇大升, 明彥, 高峰
kijil, ch'i-chih 氣質
kijil chi sŏng, ch'i-chih chih hsing 氣質之性
Kobong *see* Ki Taesŭng
Kobong chŏnsŏ 高峰全書
kwŏn, chüan 卷
Kyeham 季涵
li 理
Li T'ung, Yen-p'ing 李侗, 廷平
Liu Shu-men 劉叔文
Lo Ch'in-shun, Cheng-an 羅欽順, 整庵
Meng-tzu chi-chu 孟子集註
mu i chi 無異指
munjip 文集
Myŏngŏn *see* Ki Taesŭng
myo maek, miao-mai 苗脈
Nan-hsien *see* Chang Shih
No Susin, Sojae 盧守慎蘇齋
Pae Chongho 裵宗鎬
pi yu i ŭi 非有二義
pi yu i ŭi 非有異義
ponyŏn, pen-jan 本然
sa, ssu 私
Sa chil igi wangbok sŏ 四七理氣往復書
Sa'am 思菴
sim, hsin 心
Sŏ Kyŏngdŏk, Hwadam 徐敬德, 花潭
Sŏng Hon, Ugye 成渾, 午溪
Sŏnghak sipdo 聖學十圖
sŏngnihak 性理學

so ch'ui i ŏn cha, so chiu erh yen che 所就而言者
so chi i ŏn cha, so chih erh yen che 所指而言者
so chongnae, so ts'ung-lai 所從來
so chu 所主
so i yŏn, so yi jan 所以然
Sojae *see* No Susim
Song Ikp'il, Unjang 宋翼弼, 雲長
Sowa 小窩
Sung (dynasty) 宋
Ta hsüeh 大學
Ta hsüeh huo wen 大學或問
Ta-hsüeh chang-chü 大學章句
taesŏl, tuei-shuo 對說
T'ai chi tu 太極圖
T'ai chi tu shuo 太極圖說
tan, tuan 端
T'an kung 檀弓
T'oegye chŏnsŏ 退溪全書
T'oegye *see* Yi Hwang
tosim, tao-hsin 道心
Ts'ai Yüan-ting, Hsi-shan 蔡元定, 西山
Ts'ui-yen 粹言
Tzu Ssu 子思
Ugye *see* Sŏng Hon
Unjang *see* Song Ikp'il
Wai-shu 外書
Yen Hui 顏回
Yen-p'ing *see* Li T'ung
Yi Hwang, T'oegye 李滉, 退溪
Yi I, Yulgok 李珥, 栗谷
Yulgok *see* Yi I

Selected Bibliography

Chan, Wing-tsit. *A Source Book in Chinese Philosophy*. Princeton: Princeton University Press, 1963.

Ch'eng Hao. *Ming-tao wen-chi*. (The Collected Literary Works of Ch'eng Hao). In *Erh Ch'eng ch'üan-shu*. Ssu-pu Pei-yao, ed.

Ch'eng I. *I-ch'uan wen-chi*. (The Collected Literary Works of Ch'eng I). In *Erh Ch'eng ch'üan-shu*. Ssu-pu Pei-yao, ed.

Ch'eng Hao and Ch'eng I. *Erh Ch'eng Ch'üan-shu*. (Complete Works of the Two Ch'engs). Ssu-pu Pei-yao, ed.

———. *I-shu*. (Surviving Works). In *Erh Ch'eng ch'üan-shu*. Ssu-pu Pei-yao, ed.

———. *Ts'ui-yen*. (Pure Words). In *Erh Ch'eng ch'üan-shu*. Ssu-pu Pei-yao, ed.

———. *Wai-shu*. (Additional Works). In *Erh Ch'eng ch'üan-shu*. Ssu-pu Pei-yao, ed.

Chu Hsi. *Chung-yung chang-chü*. (Commentary on the *Doctrine of the Mean*). In *Ssu-shu wu-ching*.

———. *Chung-yung huo-wen*. (Questions and Answers on the *Doctrine of the Mean*). Seoul: Kyŏngmunsa, 1977. Photo reprint, n.d.

———. *Chu Tzu ta-ch'üan*. (The Complete Works of Master Chu). Taiwan: Cheng-chung Shu-chu, 1970. Photo reprint of Ssu-pu pei-yao, ed.

———. *Chu Tzu yü-lei*. (Classified Conversations of Master Chu). Comp. Li Ching-te. Taiwan: Cheng-chung Shu-chu, 1962. Photo reprint of 1473 ed.

203

————. *Meng Tzu chi-chu*. (Commentary on the *Mencius*). In *Ssu-shu wu-ching*.

————. *Ta-hsüeh chang-chü*. (Commentary on the *Great Learning*). In *Ssu-shu wu-ching*.

————. *Ta Hsüeh huo-wen*. (Questions and Answers on the *Great Learning*). Seoul: Kyŏngmunsa, 1977. Photo reprint, n.d.

Chu Hsi, comp. *Yen-p'ing ta-wen*. (Li T'ung's Answers to Chu Hsi's Questions). In *Ilbon gakp'an Yi T'oegye chŏnjip* (Japan edition of the works of Yi T'oegye), ed. Abe Yoshio. Seoul: T'oegyehak Yŏn'guwŏn, 1975.

Hu Kuang et al. *Hsing-li ta-ch'üan*. (The Great Compendium of Neo-Confucianism). Seoul: Kwangsŏng Munhwasa, 1975. Photo reprint, n.d. on ed.

Lee, Peter, et al. eds. *Sources of Korean Tradition*. New York: Columbia University Press, 1992.

Pae Chongho, comp. *Hanguk yuhak charyo chipsŏng*. (Compendium of Korean Confucian Materials). 3 vols. Seoul: Yŏnsei Taehakkyo Ch'ulp'anbu, 1980.

————. *Hanguk yuhaksa*. (History of Korean Confucianism). Seoul: Yŏnsei Taehakkyo Ch'ulp'anbu, 1974.

Shih-san ching chu-shu. (The Thirteen Classics with Notes and Commentary). Shanghai: Shih-chieh Shu-chü, 1935. Photolithographic reprint of 1815 ed.

Ssu shu wu ching. (The Four Books and Five Classics). Shanghai: Shih-chieh Shu-chü, 1936.

Yi Hwang. *T'oegye chŏnsŏ*. (The Complete Works of Yi Hwang). 2 vols. Seoul: Sŏnggyun'gwan Taehakkyo Taedong Munhwa Yŏnguwŏn, 1958. Photo reprint.

Yi I. *Yulgok chŏnsŏ*. 2 vols. Seoul: Sŏnggyun'gwan Taehakkyo Taedong Munhwa Yŏnguwŏn, 1958. Photo reprint.

Index

abstract, 9, 29
activation. *See* external stimulus of
animals, 128
An Sŭpji, 165, 171
anthropocosmic, xvi, xxi, xxxii, xxxiii
appetites, 151, see also desires
approach. *See* method
aroused. *See* external stimulus

blocked, xxv, 126, 127, 128. *See also*
    disruption; material force: de-
    grees of purity, turbidity, and
    coarseness; mind-and-heart:
    disruption of; physical nature;
    obstruction
body, xvi, xix, xxii, xxix, 4, 63, 97,
    128, 141, 142
Book of Rites, xxvii, 4, 33, 43, 106,
    129, 149
Book of Changes, 12, 33, 54, 133
Buddhism, xvi, xvii, xvii, xix, xxii,
    xxxi, 119, 149, 164

categorization
    in diagrams, 42
    of Four Beginnings and Seven Feel-
        ings, 45, 59, 61, 63, 82, 83,
        85, 101, 102, 142
    of human mind and Tao mind, 112,
        123, 130

of Seven Feelings as material force,
    75, 142
of nature as not exclusively material
    force, 37
See also method
chance expression, 75
Chang-chü chi-chü, 31
Chang Shih (Nan-hsien), 41
Chang Tsai (Heng-ch'ü), xvi, xxiv,
    10, 18, 51, 64, 74, 119, 128,
    142
characteristics, xxv, 6, 25, 65, 77,
    90, 160
Cheng-an. *See* Lo Ch'in-shun
Ch'eng-Chu school, xv–xxvi *passim*,
    xxxi, xxxi, 90, 125
Ch'eng brothers, xv, xvi, xvii, xix,
    xxiv, 10, 18, 27, 51, 64, 76,
    142. *See also* Ch'eng Hao;
    Ch'eng I
Ch'eng Hao (Ming-tao), xvi, 74. *See
    also* Ch'eng brothers
Ch'eng I (I-ch'uan), xvi, 27, 32, 60,
    71, 119, 43, 60, 71, 91. *See
    also* Ch'eng brothers
Ch'engs. *See* Ch'eng brothers
Ch'en Ch'i-chih, 24, 58
Ch'en Ch'un (Pei-hsi), 141, 149, 159
ch'i. See li and *ki*; material force
Ch'ing dynasty, xix

205

undifferentiated
    approach, 13, 39, 55
    way of speaking, 21, 25, 61, 63,
        64, 65, 67, 68, 69, 142
    feelings within, 30
    mind-and-heart before aroused, 43
    substance of nature, 24
    substance of principle, 73
    See also method: speaking of
unity, xxiii, xxiv, xxxi, xxxi, 12, 14,
    54, 56, 67, 119, 120, 126,
    130, 157, 176
universe, xxiv, xxvii, xxxiii, xxxiv,
    27, 85, 174
Unjang, 165
unmoving, 133

vacuous, 120
values, xv, xxxi, 110, 175
vessel of water, 150–151. See also
    simile

Wade-Giles, ix
water, 66, 67, 85, 86, 87, 91, 143,
    145, 150, 151, 152, 155, 164.
    See also simile
wave, 86. See also simile
wellspring, xvi, 147, 156, 160, 164

wholeness, 9, 51, 73
world view, xv, xxiii

Yao, the sage, 111, 120, 121
Yen Hui's Love of Learning, 13, 31,
    32, 54, 58
Yen-p'ing. See Li T'ung
Yi Hwang (T'oegye), xv, xxi, xxxiii,
    9, 26, 29, 64, 66, 71, 74, 90,
    129, 131, 167
    in Yulgok-Ugye correspondence,
        109, 110, 111, 115, 121, 133,
        137, 139, 141, 149, 150, 161,
        175, 178, 182
    See also T'oegye-Kobong debate
Yi I (Yulgok), ix, xv, xvii, xxx, xx-
    xiii, 117, 125, 129, 130, 145,
    148, 153, 154, 167, 173, 175,
    176, 179, 180. See also
    Yulgok-Ugye debate
yin and yang, 40, 84, 85, 89, 126,
    132, 147, 163, 164, 177,
Yŏnsan'gun, xx, xxi
Yu Tzu, 149
Yü-lei, xiv, 7, 14, 18, 38, 56, 58, 76,
    92, 93, 96, 97, 107, 140,
Yulgok-Ugye debate, ix, xxvi, xxx–
    xxxi, 26, 109, 110